The Relationally Intelligent Child

The Relationally Intelligent Child

Five Keys to Helping Your Kids Connect Well with Others

John Trent & Dewey Wilson

NORTHFIELD PUBLISHING

CHICAGO

Edited by Cheryl Molin
Interior design: Ragont Design
Cover design: Erik M. Peterson
Cover illustration of hands copyright © 2013 by Vectorig / iStock (183934064). All rights reserved.

Library of Congress Cataloging-in-Publication Data

Names: Trent, John, 1952- author. | Wilson, Dewey, author.
Title: The relationally intelligent child : five keys to helping your kids
   connect well with others / John Trent and Dewey Wilson.
Description: Chicago : Northfield Publishing, [2020] | Includes
   bibliographical references. | Summary: "The Relationally-Intelligent
   Child teaches parents the crucial insights of a must grasp concept:
   relational intelligence. This tool for growth and connection will not
   only change a child's life, but also a parent's own relationships.
   You'll discover five key elements that can engage and equip your child
   with skills for being relationally intelligent with family, friends, and
   others"-- Provided by publisher.
Identifiers: LCCN 2020035375 (print) | LCCN 2020035376 (ebook) | ISBN
   9780802416384 (paperback) | ISBN 9780802496249 (ebook)
Subjects: LCSH: Interpersonal relations in children. | Interpersonal
   communication in children. | Parent and child. | Parenting. |
   Parenting--Religious aspects--Christianity.
Classification: LCC BF723.I646 T74 2020 (print) | LCC BF723.I646 (ebook)
   | DDC 649/.1--dc23
LC record available at https://lccn.loc.gov/2020035375
LC ebook record available at https://lccn.loc.gov/2020035376

We hope you enjoy this book from Northfield Publishing. Our goal is to provide high-quality, thought-provoking books and products that connect truth to your real needs and challenges. For more information on other books and products that will help you with all your important relationships, go to northfieldpublishing.com or write to:

Northfield Publishing
820 N. LaSalle Boulevard
Chicago, IL 60610

1 3 5 7 9 10 8 6 4 2

Printed in the United States of America

DEDICATION FROM JOHN TRENT

To Cindy, who did so much to build love, responsibility, and relational intelligence into Kari's and Laura's lives—and now into granddaughter Zoa's life. And to our two awesome sons-in-law—Joey Stageberg and Chris Morris—for their modeling both relational intelligence and how to love their wives and family like Jesus.

DEDICATION FROM DEWEY WILSON

To my wife, Lynne, whose unwavering tenacity to raise godly children has taught me much of what I know about raising relationally intelligent children. To our children, Tiffani and Erin. For trusting Mom and Dad during those many years of swimming against the currents of mainstream culture. No greater joy do we have as parents than to witness your love for Christ be lived out in your marriages with our wonderful sons-in-law, Brian and Adam, and through our grandchildren.

Contents

Chapter 1

The Incredible Gift You Can Give a Child

As cultures across the globe continue to migrate further and further away from face-to-face friendships, love, and connection, we believe *you* can give your child an incredible gift. Current research shows no one else on the planet is better equipped to give this gift to your child than you. This gift can teach and coach your children to live out the skills needed to have positive, healthy, others-centered, world-changing, face-to-face relationships with others.

It's not a life free from challenges, stress, or trials. But it provides your children with the strength and wisdom to get up on their own after falling down and gives them a foundation for love, connection, resilience, and care. In addition, your home can be a place that is a light to your children's friends, who long to know what healthy relationships look like. Even after your children are grown and no longer living under your roof, they'll look for ways to stay attached and spend time with you. Simply stated:

We believe you can teach your children to become relationally intelligent in a way that changes not only their life—but others' lives as well!

It's long been thought that you can't *define* love with any type of certainty. For example, a 2016 article listed "36 Definitions of Love" found in the Urban Dictionary, from its being an emotion, to a decision, to simply being "undefinable"![1] But an avalanche of new clinical studies and even timeless biblical truths say otherwise. We believe it's possible for you to show your children how deeply they are loved through your everyday actions. And, as they see you demonstrate this amazing love *relationally*, you're giving them a model of how to highly value themselves and love others compassionately.

You might be wondering why we seem to be so confident. Like the noted futurists John Naisbitt and Patricia Aburdene wrote, we also believe, "The most exciting breakthroughs of the 21st century will not occur because of technology, but because of an expanding concept of what it means to be human."[2]

And wave after wave of studies today are showing just how to be fully, wonderfully, healthily human is to be *relational*! It is how we are created.

We'll introduce a more expanded definition of what we mean by being "relational" and "relationally intelligent" in the next chapter. But for now, we want you to know it's about being able to identify and value your own strengths and helping your children understand their strengths as well. It's about understanding ways to genuinely value and connect with others. It's being able to model and coach your children how to take positive risks that go with exploring their world, while also exploring what others could be thinking and feeling. Then, it's working together with your children, helping them to become more creative and resilient. It's also helping them to be linked to something greater than themselves, motivating and empowering them to go change their world for the better.

Basically, there really are applicational, relational blocks we can lay down in our child's life that are essential for building a genuine love.

In fact, this book centers around five specific elements. Each of these five are core elements in unleashing what we call *relational intelligence*. Like cracking open an atom, they generate powerful positive relational changes and benefits for your child. We'll share why these five elements make such a positive difference and surround them with hands-on examples. After you've seen them up close, we'll help you create a "starting point plan" for bringing these skills and traits into your home.

Why Is Being "Relational" That Important?

It's been thirty years now since the first personal computers and cell-phones began infiltrating almost all aspects of our everyday life. We've been dealing with technology long enough now to begin understanding the risk factors that we didn't recognize early on.

No doubt, parents from the 1950s eventually learned that smoking in a car with the windows up was damaging (or smoking in general, much less around children). Parents today, in their heart of hearts, are beginning to understand the need to put down the screen and start relating more with their children in a way that builds personal, loving relationships.

But the real challenge is how do you actually build stronger relationships with your child once you put down your phone!

The great news is that you can help your children experience and create positive relationships by learning and modeling what they need to learn in your home. In the process, you'll discover how they learn and how prepared they are for real-world experiences like relating well with others in the workplace, social settings, and even their loving relationships in the future. Becoming relationally intelligent will have a positive impact on their health and future.

Consider an eye-opening study out of UNC–Chapel Hill showing your children's *life expectancy* is linked with their ability to be relational.[3] Drawing on the research of four major studies concerning health and longevity, the lack of close-knit, face-to-face relationships is now actively linked with high blood pressure, abdominal obesity, heart disease, stroke, and even cancer risk! Conversely, these negative physical measures all go down as you help your child experience and learn to build close relationships and friendships. Talk about a gift that keeps on giving! *You are giving them life when you teach them to be relationally intelligent.*

Yes, there are significant benefits to having screen-based relationships. We're not asking you to ceremonially smash your smartphone here at the start of this book. But what we *are* asking you to do is take time to learn how to build healthy relationships by being willing to first put down that digital screen. When you do, you're not only benefiting your health and that of your children, but you are also influencing the imprint of their perspective on whether they had a "happy" or "unhappy" childhood.

A new study on childhood memories found the memories most linked with a happy childhood didn't involve how many major vacations or "cool experiences" parents provided for their children, nor the number of "things" they were given.[4] Being happy in childhood wasn't even linked to the absence of negative or difficult experiences. Instead, emotional happiness was linked to the very same thing that impacts their physical health: *the degree of connected, caring relationships in their home!*

The quality of your children's relationship with *you* at home is more important than any cruise or theme park trip. The memories of individuals who knew they were deeply loved and cared for as children, even in a less-than-perfect home with failures and challenges (like most of ours), are the happiest and most remembered in adulthood.

One final benefit for now (and we'll share many more throughout the book) is how applying relational intelligence in your home effectively battles the #1 health risk for children and adults today. It isn't the terrible, dreaded disease of cancer. Instead, more people are suffering from *a cancerous lack of relationships*, which leads to loneliness!

In a University of Chicago study,[5] loneliness was shown to cause dramatic increases in the stress hormone cortisol, which is linked with hardening of the arteries and inflammation. Loneliness was also shown to diminish executive functioning, memory, and learning. The bottom line is, better than any statin pill, these researchers' prescription for helping your children learn more effectively and have better health as well is you spending time helping them build their relational networks—and not just with TikTok, Facebook friends, Instagram followers, or online gamer friends from down the street or across the country. According to these studies, those online "friends" and "relationships" didn't erase loneliness, as much as we might wish they did. It is *face-to-face relationships* with friends and family like you that move a child away from loneliness!

Does it sound like we're giving loneliness too much credit for damaging lives? If so, check this out.

In England, the degree of damage to public health linked to loneliness has become so pronounced, British prime minister Theresa May appointed the first "Minister of Loneliness" to help with all the health and mental challenges. Japan is facing an exploding epidemic of *kodokushi*. Roughly translated, it means "lonely deaths." And it's not just older people but young people as well!

People in Germany, Scandinavia, and France have more money, are better educated, and have better health care than at any time in their history. But in every one of those countries—as well as America—young people are *unhappier* than at any time since the process of collecting data began.

Here in the United States, studies show that the majority of people today say they have either one or zero close friends—down from three or four just a few decades ago.

So, why are we so lonely?

We know that in our crazy-busy world, full of "stranger danger" warnings and scary real-life challenges, for us and our children to take the risk to get out and make friends isn't always easy. And what about busyness? You and everyone you know are incredibly busy. It seems like if we don't take the time to match schedules with people in our lives, we tend to find ourselves spending more time online, texting, emailing, or having video chats with these same people than intentionally taking time to build face-to-face, personal relationships.

It is easier—and it can seem "safer"—to just click our fingers on a keyboard to do relationships. A click of a finger can register a "like," or two thumbs can share 280 characters in a flash. We can even join an online group. But frankly, if we never meet up with that group through face-to-face interaction, then it doesn't matter what we call our Facebook group.

Becoming relationally intelligent through face-to-face, in-person relationships is harder than posting a perfect social media picture or selfie. However, it is also immeasurably more beneficial to your children when you teach them how to engage, explore, love, serve, and relate well with real people!

We Are "Wired" for Relationships

There are undisputable realities of *why* you and your child need personal, face-to-face relationships, and why skipping out on being the coach and guide to your children is not an option. Most of us already know that we need help putting down the technology and guidance for knowing how to gain new skills in building stronger personal relationships. Most of us parents know we need to be the ones modeling relational connection for our children.

Let's go back to the great news we have to share with you, not only in this book but also online at therelationallyintelligentchild.com— the news that doing relationships well is something you are already wired by your Creator to do!

As you learn more about these five applicational building blocks of relational intelligence and begin applying them in your home, you'll be amazed at the confidence you gain in face-to-face relationships. And as you strengthen your family's attachment bonds in the process, you'll discover yourself gaining an amazing internal balance.

Pick a sport. If you're going to be a great athlete, balance is a key to success in any one of them. Relationally, we can learn to have inner balance that helps us wisely move toward others as parents, spouses, and friends. Balance that motivates us to add adventure and creativity to our life. To help us stand up after we get knocked down. To embrace love from others and know how to love and value others. *Even if they're different than us.* And yes, even in a world that is incredibly polarized. We want to help you and your children embrace a more positive future—amidst all of life's challenges.

So, think about that long list of benefits you've just read.

You and your child becoming better at relationships. Each of you experiencing better health. Happier memories. More friendships. Less loneliness. Less exposure to the "second-hand smoke" of excessive screen time. Gaining that inner balance to reach out and be resilient and carry with you a positive view toward the future—even when we're living in times of great trials.

Who doesn't want that for their children or for themselves!

Let's get started, then, by gaining a picture and a definition of what it means to live out those five key relationally intelligent elements.

Chapter 2

What Is Relational Intelligence?

To begin our understanding of relational intelligence, let's walk into a "brick and mortar" store that virtually everyone is familiar with, an Apple Store. Yes, even if you're a PC fan, it's worth walking inside, even for just a moment.

When you do, from our experiences, you'll be walking into a place filled with people from opening to close. Displays everywhere pulse with light and energy and the atmosphere is often crazy with noise. Typically, you'll find classes being held somewhere in the store, full of people of all ages learning how to use the latest technology from slides being projected on a wall. And of course, lots of sales for Apple.

You'd think the key to all this excitement would be that the sales-people spend countless hours learning how to master every detail and every update on the iPhone, every model of Mac computer, and every generation of iPad throughout the store. If so, you'd be wrong. Although these "frontline" Apple employees are very well trained, what you've just walked into is a living, breathing example of applied relational intelligence.[1]

Even the Apple "geniuses," those experts in the back who master technical challenges, repairs, and troubleshooting every problem, are generally good at relationships. Their ability to speak tech-talk to the average person leaves most of us feeling a little more intelligent when we walk out the door.

From our perspective, what you are really being sold when you walk in is an experience and a relationship.[2] That's because the first and largest group of people you meet in the front of the store, with the colored T-shirts and almost certain smiles, are the Apple *specialists*. They are people like my (John's) friend Mark, who has worked at an Apple Store now for several years.

Mark was in his sixties and knew virtually nothing about smartphones and personal computers when he walked into his first Apple Store. He had, however, had a very successful career in running a local "mom and pop" bookstore for decades. (Think the "Shop Around the Corner" in the classic movie with Meg Ryan and Tom Hanks.) But as book sales went to big chains and then to online sales, small bookstores everywhere closed up. That caused him to lose his store, retire earlier than he wanted, and quickly become very bored.

Then he got a new Apple computer and he ran into a problem understanding something about it. So he walked into an Apple Store near his home for advice. He was quickly met by someone in a colored shirt who listened to and solved his problem in a blink. But as a former store owner, what amazed him was the warmth and life and energy that seemed to spring from the person he talked to, as well as the people with the same color T-shirt throughout the store. So he said to the person helping him, "Do you ever hire old people like me?"

"Absolutely!" said the Apple specialist who had helped him and who turned out to be one of the store managers.

"But I know almost nothing about phones and computers," Mark said.

"That's OK," the manager told him. "What we're looking for are people with great relationship skills. If that's you, we can teach you the details." Which they did, and he puts his outstanding relational skills into action still today. He used to charm people, talk about the book they needed, or point them toward a resource for that problem they were trying to solve. He once used relationships to point people toward a book. Now he does the same thing with technology.

Relational Rating Is Everywhere

Today, pick almost any area in the business sector and you'll see how it's being driven to be more "relational." For example, let's say you're not feeling great. It's been several days, and now it's time to go to a clinic. With healthcare moving closer to where people live, urgent care centers are popping up in many drugstores, supermarkets, and corner shopping centers.

You would think that technology and clinical expertise would be the thing people value most about their experience. And indeed, most urgent care centers have a topnotch NP (nurse practitioner) or PA (physician's assistant), an x-ray tech, a med tech, and a receptionist out front. They offer a multitude of tests that give you "right now" results, everything from strep tests to heart tests. But while people *expect* the latest clinical tests and medical expertise, what they *value most* is something they can understand. *Relationships!*

Ask the NPs or PAs who staff these centers what really matters. You'll learn it's not just their wise diagnosis and treatment. What's crucial to the rating that the clinic and the provider gets is the *experience* a person had relationally.

From meeting the med tech out front to the nurse practitioner in the back, the number of stars they give on the survey tends to reflect the way they believe they were treated relationally. And those stars (or their equivalent) can impact a provider's bonus or career. Meaning, *on top of* all their medical skills, they must have relational skills as well—which are not always taught in NP and PA schools!

Pick almost any job today and you'll see the same thing. Almost every business now is being driven by customer service and relationships. We demand relational intelligence from baristas and bank tellers. It's a key component for how we choose roofers and whether we return a second time to the place our car was repaired. However, most people who work in these places will go through an entire educational or vocational career without a single class on how to do relationships well. We just assume people already know how to relate with each other. Yet there's no training on doing relationships well from grade school through trade or graduate school. Sadly, those life-skills classes were removed from many schools along with home economics and art classes.

What's the result? People are clamoring for skills at relating.

For example, at UC Berkeley, more than seventy students couldn't get into a new, every-seat-full "adulting" class. The following semester, more than two hundred students signed up for the same class and more than half of them were turned away. This was a course not just on life skills such as how to create a budget, but primarily filled with coaching on how to do relationships in the real world. The same thing is true at the Adulting School in Portland, Maine, where classes are bursting at the seams.[3]

All across this country, young men and women in colleges and graduate schools are actively seeking help in filling up something they've missed in home and school. It's those core skills on doing life and relationships well that we'll be coaching you on in this book.

One More "American Picking Good" Example of Relational Intelligence

Let's look at one more example of where you can see applied relational intelligence being demonstrated. Pickers are people who spend their time searching for antiques and unique items they can purchase and resell to others. Arguably, the most famous "pickers" on the planet are Mike Wolfe, Frank Fritz, and Danielle Colby . They are the stars of the hit show *American Pickers*, which has run for over twenty consecutive seasons.

Watching episodes of *American Pickers*, we see how Mike and Frank *value* and build attachment with the people they're talking to. We watch them step right into people's lives and be interested in and value them as *people,* linking what they've done with something bigger, like preserving history or treasuring or continuing a loved one's interests or legacy.

With these examples, we hope you're beginning to get a picture of how, even in our day of amazing technological advances, it's *relationships* that hook us, encourage us, motivate us, and inspire us. And it is relationships driven by relational intelligence that will build great things into the life of your child!

How "Relational" Ability Is Different from "Capacity" Learning

As we unpack more closely what relational intelligence is, it's important to know up front that this kind of relational skill isn't reserved for certain personalities. We're not saying you have to be born with the relational skills of a top Apple Store associate. Or be skilled at getting total strangers to open their doors and storage sheds like Mike and Frank. We can all learn a great deal about relating well with others— no matter our natural personality. And as we learn how to better relate to others, we'll also be able to teach and model relational wisdom to our own children.

Why are we so confident about you being able to do that? In large part, it's because we believe you have the innate intelligence to impact your child's life relationally.

Let's start by digging into that word, *intelligence.*

We're sure you've heard the term "artificial intelligence" (even though it's often linked incorrectly to movies based on mad robots taking over from humans). Or perhaps you're familiar with "business intelligence," where we're told we can transform how business information is collected, integrated, analyzed, and presented.[4] And who hasn't heard about the concept of "emotional intelligence"? Appropriately understanding our emotions is an incredibly powerful tool for doing life well with others.

Experts are doing great work on the clinical and research-based aspects of connecting emotional skills with relationship skills. For example, we're very grateful for Dr. Gary Oliver and his outstanding work on linking EI (emotional intelligence) and RI (relational intelligence) at John Brown University's Relationship Center.

But in almost every case, when you hear the word *intelligence*, it's being looked at as a "capacity" measurement. Here's what we mean. I (Dewey) was in elementary and junior high school with identical twin brothers. Each of them was an exact replica of the other, making it virtually impossible to distinguish them. Their own mother had trouble sorting them out, so playing pranks on our teachers was easy for them.

The thing I remember most, however, was how incredibly intelligent they both were. I'm pretty sure when we were in kindergarten, they were conjugating verbs while the rest of us struggled with learning to spell one syllable words. I know for a fact they graduated first and second among their class in college with degrees in nuclear engineering. Eventually they became bosses to a lot of the same guys who called them "nerds" in school. Talk about poetic justice!

When you think of the word *intelligent* or *intelligence*, it's most likely linked to people like these identical twin brothers, Bill Gates, Stephen Hawking, or Katherine Johnson (the NASA math expert pictured in the movie *Hidden Figures*). All of them became outstanding in business, technology, or science and were able to hold in their minds a huge capacity for detailed thoughts, facts, and figures. That is where most clinical measures of intelligence are based.

If you have ever taken an IQ test, or an ACT or SAT to get into college, then you've been exposed to broad capacity-based measurements of intelligence. In these types of measurements, capacity refers to volume, meaning there is a maximum amount that something can hold or contain, making it possible for whatever is in the container to be measured.

Regarding intelligence, it is a concept that was popular among many early psychologists and neuroscientists, mainly because they believed the *amount* of intelligence an individual possessed was *fixed* for that person. However, the amount also varied with each person.

Intelligence then, if looked at as a "capacity" measure, could be quantified. We could even assign people some level of intelligence quotient, a higher quotient reflecting a greater level of "smartness" possessed by the individual.

But our focus and definition in using the word *intelligence* is not about *capacity*! Our goal isn't to help you or your child gain or even measure your broad base of general knowledge. Nor is it based on the idea that there's a cap on your ability to acquire knowledge or to develop characteristic traits helpful for creating new relationships. In fact, you'll soon read an entire section on amazing new findings in neuroscience showing that our brains actually can learn and apply something new, regardless of our age or background, therefore blowing up the "cap" theory of our ability to acquire knowledge!

What we're laying out with our definition of relational intelligence is an *ability-based, applicational* understanding of this phrase. How you can gain tools, examples, and insights to apply when relating and connecting closely with others. How you can model relational intelligence with your children as they watch you *apply* these relational skills as a parent and person!

Intelligence's Applicational Link to Wisdom

Depending on the translation, the word *wisdom* is found in the Bible some 216 times. Almost forty times it's found in the book of Proverbs alone. "How much better it is to get wisdom than gold!" (Prov. 16:16), and "For wisdom is better than jewels; and all desirable things cannot compare with her" (8:11).

Dr. Bruce Waltke, noted Dallas Theological Seminary Semitic scholar, once shared a classic definition of wisdom as being "skill of living." That is the real-world skill of doing relationships well that we'll be focusing on in this book. In other words, we're challenging and guiding people to be relationally intelligent as they apply and live out a certain set of core skills for doing life well.

Even the *Merriam-Webster* dictionary defines intelligence as "the *ability* to learn or understand . . . the *ability* to *apply* knowledge to manipulate one's environment."[4]

Likewise, the *Collins English Dictionary* defines intelligence as "the ability to think, reason, and understand instead of doing things automatically or by instinct." And the Apple Dictionary states intelligence is "the ability to acquire and apply knowledge."

With that in mind, here's our definition of relational intelligence: *relational intelligence is exercising our natural ability to learn, understand, and apply healthy relationship skills needed for successfully connecting and interacting with others.*

> *Relational intelligence is exercising our natural ability to learn, understand, and apply healthy relationship skills needed for successfully connecting and interacting with others.*

We'll dive deeper into each aspect of this definition as we go through the book. But just know that we believe you already have the God-given, "uncapped" *ability* (not capacity) to understand and *apply* wise, relational living. You can learn to do relationships well, even in a world where so many people and situations seek to put a "cap" on who you are today or can become tomorrow.

We also want you to know the goal for acquiring relational intelligence is never to exert control, nor to gain any advantage over anyone or any situation that could harm or defraud another individual. If your primary focus for getting better at relationships is so you can control or use other people, it will eventually ruin every relationship you have. Our goal for teaching you these skills is for you and your children to experience a new level of love, lived out well by applying five key elements of relational intelligence.

Where did these five elements come from? We have had the privilege of working with couples and families for more than sixty years combined. Dr. Wilson's PhD is in cognitive learning with his dissertation focused on relational commitment among millennials. Dr. Trent's doctorate is in marriage and family therapy, and his dissertation was on what builds attachment in caring, bonded relationships with children.

We both teach in graduate programs and have done decades of study and research on family interactions. In doing so, we have quantified these five elements as being core measures of what is constantly seen in high-functioning, strongly attached, healthy children and parents—what we refer to as relational intelligence.

Now that's not to say there aren't other aspects of doing relationships wisely and well that could have been factored in. After studying and researching healthy family functioning, other traits can certainly move under the heading of one of these five core elements that we've isolated and focused on.

For example, you won't see "compassion" as one of the key measures. But it's closely linked with the fifth element of relational intelligence for children, which is Future-Focused Service. Another is "courage." You'll discover it is a part of the second, third, and fourth elements. Simply put, the five elements we've chosen are broad enough to be core reflections, yet not so wide as to not be significant.

Throughout the book, you will often see us refer to the URL www. therelationallyintelligentchild.com. This website is where you will be able to find a plethora of information, insights, and additional research about parenting and other meaningful relationships you have. We'll give you more information about this later, but for now, let's lay out a map of the rest of the book.

The Five Elements of
Relational Intelligence for Parents

So much of what we do in life occurs progressively, or in succession. For example, God designed us physically to crawl before we walk, and to walk before we run. Likewise, children also learn language progressively by starting with one syllable words before learning multiple syllable words and their meaning. These small humans now have a vocabulary—a filing cabinet, if you will, full of the words they'll use to express their views over the course of a lifetime. Simply stated, God means for our children to develop progressively through a natural order.

The five elements of relational intelligence listed below are also progressive in that each element is foundational for the one that follows. In the same way it is virtually impossible for your child to run a race without first learning to walk, we'll demonstrate how developing a secure attachment with your child is foundational to every other element. A secure attachment encourages and enables them to fearlessly explore their world! Because they're going to fall when they explore, through getting up and going again, they develop an unwavering resilience as a child. All of which leads to them making wise decisions and having a future-focused perspective for serving others as teenagers and adults.

- *1st Element—The foundational need for SECURE ATTACHMENT*
- *2nd Element—Which paves a way for fostering FEARLESS EXPLORATION*
- *3rd Element—Resulting in an UNWAVERING RESILIENCE that's needed to overcome real-world relational challenges*
- *4th Element—Which becomes the platform for WISE DECISION-MAKING that's essential and crucial for developing self-regulation*
- *5th Element—With the end goal of seeing life so hopeful, it empowers FUTURE-FOCUSED SERVING of others.*

In the next chapter, we'll begin walking you through each of the five core elements and how each applies to relational intelligence. Then, once you've gone through these five core relational elements, our goal isn't to just say, "Well, good luck with that!" Instead, we're going to help you apply these principles in the following ways:

- In chapter 8, we'll help you create a starting point plan for bringing relational intelligence into your unique home and family.

- We'll look at three things that can block us from becoming relationally intelligent.

- We'll also look at three things that empower our learning and application of each element.

- Finally, we'll end the book with a challenge to pick one other family and share with them what you've learned, helping them become relationally intelligent.

Chapter 3

The First Element of Relational Intelligence: Secure Attachment

As we begin to focus on five core elements of relational intelligence, it's fair to ask the question: "Why these five?" And even more, how do these traits, if focused on, differ from just good parenting advice?

In answering the first question, based on years of observation and research on child cognition, relational awareness, and its application, these five are what we call "atomic" elements. Crack these open in your home, and they move to empower connection with other attributes of relational intelligence. Each is indeed a part of "good parenting advice." But in the "Focus and Impact" chart below, we'll share ways this chain reaction can impact a child's relational intelligence.

FOCUSING ON SECURE ATTACHMENT IMPACTS YOUR CHILD'S ABILITY TO:

- *Connect with strangers in a healthy way*
- *Place high value on others*
- *Generate greater self-confidence in new situations*
- *Regulate emotions around rejection or loss*
- *Become more sensitive to the emotions of others*
- *Activate the ability to analyze, interpret, and accurately assign meaning to others' body language*

Three Crucial Questions— Three Timeless Answers

Many of us have fond memories of our summer vacations, even though it seemed like summer flew by and school was starting again. In a positive way, we'd like you to look at these next several chapters like that first day of school. Not because we're "fun killers," but because if ever there was a time for parents to "go to school" on these five applicational elements of relational intelligence, it's today.

As you remember from school, you didn't learn everything about a subject on that first day of class. But if you had a helpful professor or teacher, you did walk out of day one with a clear picture of what the class would look like over the whole semester and maybe even how it could be of use to you in the future. If so, you probably walked out motivated and thinking, *This could be a really good class!*

That's our goal for you. Although none of these chapters are

written to be the "last and only word" on each topic, we strongly believe each one of them can be a great starting point for you and your
child becoming relationally intelligent. We have put a list of suggested
additional resources in an appendix.

In every chapter, we're going to lay out a case for why we think one
of the following five elements is essential, a reflection of what you see
in highly relational families. After explaining the concept, we'll highlight practical ways you can begin applying that element in your home.
Applicational ideas can help you build out your "starting point plan."

One more important thing before we're done with the "starting
school" analogy. In a traditional class, once the semester or the year is
finished, you're likely not to see your teacher or professor again. Hopefully that doesn't happen here. Our goal is that after you've read the
rest of this book, you'll be motivated to stay connected to learn more
about relational intelligence through our website!

You can find us coaching, guiding, and working to add to your knowledge base and applicational skills at therelationallyintelligentchild.com.
There you'll find our blog and a place to ask more specific questions. You
can listen to our podcasts, link to outstanding experts, and find other
tools online. Although this book is targeted to parents, we fully expect
singles or grandparents, people in all phases of life, to realize how important relationships can be.

For example, you'll also find more specific ideas online to support
grandparents who are doing full-time parenting. We also encourage
single parents as they face "double-duty" challenges, and highlight
ideas for adoptive families and blended families looking to apply relational intelligence. These are all important groups of parents, so if
you're in one of these categories of parenting, you can find more detailed information on our website. We'll keep highlighting new studies we think are outstanding. In addition, our website is a place where
we'll ask for and post "we did it" stories from parents just like you
whose families are currently living out one or more of the five elements
of relational intelligence.

But like day one in school, it all starts here with the first element of relational intelligence. So let's get to class and begin looking at something so life-changing we need to firmly grab hold of and consistently apply it in our home: *attachment.*

What's "Attachment" Got to Do with It?

We're going to jump into looking at examples from history and research regarding this important word shortly. Before we do, we want you to think about an "experiment" on attachment you've probably already conducted in your own home. All you need is a three- or four-year-old and something very important to him or her, like a stuffed animal.

For Kari, the Trents' older daughter, it was Sugar the blue dinosaur. For Laura, their younger daughter, it was a doll she very creatively named Cindy Mommy Trent Doll. In order to run this in-home experiment, begin by looking at that stuffed animal, toy, or doll that your child has given a special name, carries everywhere, sleeps with, expects to be buckled in together in the car seat, refuses to let you wash (unless the child is asleep), and thinks is without a peer.

Wait until your child is very tired or needs some emotional support, and then walk over and unexpectedly pull that loved one out of their hands. Actually, you should probably just *think* about doing that.

We're not asking you to literally do your own study on separation anxiety or what clinical attachment researchers title "primal panic." But if you've ever lost a "Sugar the dinosaur" or its equivalent that your child is deeply attached to, you can literally see the inner emotional panic they experience. And yes, for a child, it doesn't have to be a real person. Even a personified and deeply loved stuffed animal or beloved pet can set off inner alarm bells in a child's heart if it's suddenly taken away.

Let's look at several reasons why this is true for children *and* adults. Let's see why attachment is so real to human beings, even at the earliest ages. In doing so, we'll also see why living out and applying attachment needs to be a key part of how you teach relational intelligence to your children.

A Brief History of Attachment

This word *attachment* first became a subject of serious study at the end of World War II. Depending on the source you consult, at least 70 million people, counting both soldiers and civilians, died in that epic war. To gain a picture of the scope of such a loss, think about seven hundred Super Bowl stadiums full of people snatched away from their families and futures.

In the aftermath of so much loss, particularly in Europe, the number of orphaned children was staggering. Many countries tried to rally and help these sometimes physically and always emotionally wounded and abandoned children. The World Health Organization commissioned a study of European children left homeless and orphaned by the conflict.

The lead researcher was an Englishman named John Bowlby. He looked at the effects on children with severe emotional and physical deprivation. Not just their toys pulled away, but their primary sources of love and attachment, their parents, now gone. What he found led to the first clinical studies and important insights on what is now called *attachment.*

Bowlby concluded that just to *survive* and grow up in a healthy way, children desperately needed someone to reach back to them when they reached out, someone in their life they could rely on to help them deal with life's emotions. Someone who saw value in them and did their best to communicate their commitment to stay with them as they grew up.

In presenting his conclusions to the British Psychoanalytic Society, and later to the Royal Society of Medicine in London, Bowlby was jeered at, nearly thrown out of the assemblies, and roundly shamed and discredited. After all, it was "settled science" at the time that all that closeness, caring, and commitment being lavished on a child would just turn that boy or girl into a clingy, overdependent snowflake of their day, a hysterical tyrant. It was "known" by everyone who was anyone of stature that you needed to keep a "professional distance"

between you and your child. You were to step away from your children
if they reached out too much. *Even if they were emotionally hurting or
afraid.* To do otherwise was thought to cripple them emotionally, leaving them without the ability to be resilient.

That kind of thinking ruled in those days and, unfortunately, for
many more days to come. For example, as late as the 1960s, parents
were only allowed to visit a sick, hurting child in the hospital (even
a two-year-old) for one hour a *week* in the US and Britain.[1] (Think
about that rule if you had a small child in the hospital today.)

Finally, clinical studies began to pile up that were so clear, so com-
pelling, that medical and psychological gatekeepers had to take notice.
Study after study began clearly showing that it wasn't emotionally and
physically "stepping away" from a child that kept him or her from emotional harm. *It was the main cause for it!*

We won't go into historical detail on all the groundbreaking
studies by Bowlby and other attachment researchers like Ainsworth,
Harlow, and Robertson, but it finally became clinically irrefutable that
being strongly connected with your children brought them health, life,
resilience, and freedom. Not the reverse. *But why?*

It turned out children who were loved and strongly attached to a
parent (or significant parent figure) *were the least likely* to show over-
dependence, truancy, anxiety, anger, and disengagement. In almost
every case, those negative traits were coming from children who
had been denied attachment. And more studies began to show that
it wasn't just orphans of war or trauma who were negatively affected.
Some children were "orphans at home." Their parents provided the
physical basics, but for whatever reason chose to step away verbally
and emotionally when their child reached out for them.

In some cases, like death or a terribly acrimonious divorce, a
parent stepping away from a child is unwanted but unavoidable. But
those same feelings of "primal panic" at the physical loss of a parent
can be seen in children of a parent who is physically present but emotionally absent. With parents who choose to emotionally ignore or
not be present for their children. Children who grow up in a home

characterized by distance, disinterest, constant distraction, or broken-ness from a parent who doesn't reach back, miss crucial life lessons on how to attach to not just their parents, but others!

Many parents simply don't know how important it is to respond to their children. To engage with them. To set down the phone, make good eye contact, and listen to them. It may be especially difficult if their own parents were too busy or unwilling to do so. Or, more recently, if for much of their lives they've been engrossed in a digital screen gaming or communicating on social media. Maybe this is great when it comes to multitasking, but a child needs our undivided attention.

Our children need to grow up in a home where when they reach out to us, we *see* what they're doing and reach back. That choice can usher in incredible benefits for them.

Attachment science started with a few groundbreaking studies in Bowlby's day. Today, the studies coming out about the benefits of building a close connection with your child are numerous. One in-sightful homework assignment could be to find a friend who has online access to a good college or research library. Have that person type the word *attachment* into any academic database. The results that spill out are like pulling a boat close to Niagara Falls and looking up. There is simply an overwhelming, drenching cascade of insightful, powerful studies coming out on attachment—as well as the negative effects of its absence.

But attachment, connection, reaching back to others who are reaching out to us, is so countercultural in our day! As we've said earlier, it's become the "second-hand smoke" of our day to just do re-lationships online, not face-to-face. Yet it's crucial to know that for many decades, something in culture has told parents they don't have to literally, physically, and emotionally reach back to a child!

In Bowlby's day, he was fighting against a professional and medi-cal culture that said "professional distance" was how to really love a child. Today, we're living with a culture where technology says, "It's OK to take a step back." But stepping back also means it needs to be done logically and realistically. For example, since the 1960s, much of culture has insisted that people can be anything they want . . . *except* "codependent!"

It is ingrained in the popular mind now that we should never let someone else rule over our life, make our decisions for us, trample on our "right" to do whatever we want to do. *We absolutely agree those aren't good things—and that there is such a thing as unhealthy dependency.* No one should let another person trample over them. But the fact is that it's the children who have grown up emotionally abandoned and unattached to their parents who are the *most likely* to step into unhealthy codependent relationships as adults.

Healthy connection is not codependency! There is such a thing as *healthy dependency.* It's healthy when our children reach out to us, expressing their need for us to comfort them, and when they look for our encouragement or our words of praise when they jump off the diving board for the first time or almost score a goal in soccer. It's also healthy for us to take the time and effort to acknowledge their needs when they reach out to us, then reach back to them when they're hurting emotionally or tired and frustrated. When combined with sound discipline and instruction, these connections are not only foundational for them learning and living out relational intelligence as children, but they also empower them to one day teach them to their children.

A wonderful picture of this healthy parental connection is seen in Scripture when Moses reminded and encouraged parents to completely love God and His Word above all else, then to diligently teach God's principles and commands to their children and model God's love at all times (Deut. 6:5–9), constantly training them in the way God would have them go so they wouldn't depart from what they learned when they were old (Prov. 22:6). As marriage and family counselors, we have heard the heartache and unfulfilled longing of far too many people who have never heard even once, much less repeatedly, that they are loved, special, valuable, and have great worth in what they share and do!

Children who grow up with a strong attachment to even *one* loving parent or loving caregiver have far higher scores in traits like resilience, thriving, self-regulation, healthy risk-taking, physical health, and service to others. These are only a few on a long list of positives! But it all stems from a choice the parent or parents made to initiate healthy connection with their children, blessing them with spoken words and meaningful touches, consistently attaching high value to them (all unique blessings we'll talk about later), and reaching back when their children reached out to them. That does not mean you have to give in to your child demanding a toy in the grocery store. Or that you should never take a second for yourself. Or that you and your spouse quit your date nights or game nights with friends. You need attachment with your spouse and friends as well. But while you can outsource the washing of your windows, your dry cleaning, even preparation of your taxes, you cannot outsource your children's attachment to *you*. Attachment is the platform you build beneath them that greatly influences whether they are going to do well or poorly at relationships.

Our impatience tends to easily show up in marriage. At the end of the day, we have to slow down and think about our spouse by setting aside our selfishness in order to talk through issues and make healthy decisions. Like marriage, parenting will absolutely show us how selfish we are. Yet for anything you sacrifice, we believe you'll be rewarded ten times over as you see your child grow up with a strong sense of healthy attachment.

Attachment Meets a
Crucial Need in All Our Lives

So, if attachment is so important to our children, at what age do they outgrow that need for connection with a few significant others? Laying aside Methuselah's great age for the moment, in modern history, the Frenchwoman Jeanne Calment (1875–1997) holds the current verified record for being the longest-lived person at 122 years, 164 days. We'd say that day 165 plus 122 years is about the time your child—or you—doesn't need human attachment!

As powerful as attachment is to a child, studies are multiplying on the incredible benefits of *adult* bonding. Most notably, EFT (emotionally focused therapy) has stepped in and generated a tremendous amount of research and training concerning adult attachment.

Championed by Sue Johnson, whom we quoted in the first chapter, the positive effect EFT is having on hurting couples is so drastic, it is statistically and observationally staggering. The heart of what they do, even with extremely hurting couples, is to emotionally help each partner increase their attachment to the other.

It's basically undisputable today, in more than one hundred well-documented studies, that adults as well as children deeply need to be "attached." We need people we can keep close. And we need people who are committed to staying close to us, physically and emotionally. It's not selfish to know that as you become more relationally intelligent and learn more about attachment with your child, that knowledge can spill over and benefit you and your social networks all your life as well.

We'll let you explore and learn more about childhood, adult, and couple attachment by visiting our website (which links to a number of other current and historical resources). But our focus in this book is on parents and children—and on *you* doing your own good work in laying down this foundational element of relational intelligence in your home.

Although we urge you to keep "going to school" on the history and amazing benefits of attachment for each of us at every age, let's get practical about implementing this first element as a parent. In doing so, we need to start by answering three immensely important questions. These are core attachment questions that every child, and parent, needs to answer.

Three Basic Questions of Attachment

One way to move from insight to application of attachment is to personally come to grips with three crucial questions about *your* early experience with that word. Here is an exercise we're asking you to complete based on three important questions regarding *your* past. Know as you begin, your children are formulating their answers to these same questions right now based on the way attachment is being lived out in your home. But for now, let's take a step back . . .

Think back to when you were ten years old.

If that draws a bit of a blank, that was roughly when you were in fifth grade.

Take a moment to get a mental picture of the house or apartment you were living in at the time. Picture that you're standing outside your home close enough to look in the windows. Looking into windows is allowed—it's your home. And if you need to be able to "float" in your mind's eye to get up to the third floor of your condominium to look in, that's allowed as well.

Picture every window is lit up. The rooms are not only full with every relative living with you, but also all those really close relatives and special friends you had when you were ten. (Like that "aunt" who really wasn't related to you but did so much to encourage you and form who you've become.)

From where you stand, you can see these people milling around, like after a dinner or at a party. People are walking up and interacting with you. Or walking away or right past you, too busy to notice you. As you stand and look in those windows, think about how you would answer the three questions below.

Please take your time. It may be helpful to write down your answers. Even if you purposely walked away from that home years ago and haven't looked back, these are important questions to answer now that you're a parent yourself. Even if the answers aren't what you wish they'd have been, they're important to consider in how they can still be influencing how you deal with attachment in your home today. If you need to, pray for the courage to take an honest look back.

Windows of the Soul—When I was 10 years old . . .

1. In my home, who reached back to me when I reached out for love, help, or support?

2. Who took time to try to listen to me and deal with me in a healthy way, even when I was emotional?
3. Who saw great value in me and did their best to be committed to me no matter what?

If you're like most of us, answering those questions can be an emotional journey. These questions can be like looking into a window of the soul. They look into the deepest part of who we are.

Hopefully, in your mind's eye at least one person quickly popped into sight. Someone who stepped toward you. A person whose name may well have shown up in your answer to each of those three questions.

Or perhaps your experience was very different and much more difficult. That can be particularly true if you're from the kind of home where being honest about emotions and memories wasn't practiced. Or allowed. Like if you grew up in a home (or culture) where it was considered disloyal or dishonoring to say anything negative about someone in our past.

We understand, if there are few or no names that you've written down, this was a difficult assignment. But it's a crucial one. Those three crucial questions above are an expanded version of the three questions that attachment science says each of us must answer:

1. Was someone there to reach back when you reached out?
2. Was someone willing to take the time to hear and value your emotions?
3. Was there someone in your home who saw in you great value, and did their best to stay committed to you, no matter what?

If we're serious about being relationally intelligent, then we need to first confront those three questions in our own life. Our hope is you came up with a name or, even better, names of several people who chose to live out an unshakable, positive connection with you.

You may have felt alone or "invisible" as you walked around your ten-year-old house. You may still be hurting or feel distant from those who were supposed to connect closely with you—so you chose not to answer these questions. If so, no wonder you're struggling with this idea of attachment. It's difficult to model something we never saw modeled for us!

Please know this: If you missed out on seeing "attachment" up close and personal, you do *not* have to live out the rest of your life as damaged goods!

Even if someone wasn't there at that key time in your life, at the time we are beginning to form a foundational view of ourselves, you can reverse the hurt! That reversal is done through connection and attachment. It's done by having people in your life today who can give you a new answer to what you missed in the past.

Someone like a "Drake." Drake is an important part of Angel's story. Angel was born with a cleft palate and other physical challenges. Listen to her words about her past. Even more, look at the difference having even one friend in her life who was committed and attached to her has made . . .

> *As much as I hate to admit it, I tend to be a little anxious in relationships as I'm afraid of being a burden to those I love. When I was young, my dad had a pretty short fuse and would get easily frustrated with my nearly constant needs. I felt ashamed every time I had an accident, etc. Things are better now, but I still feel anxious and somewhat insecure at times, in romantic relationships especially. However, 11 years ago, the Lord brought Drake into my life. He has called me out on each one of my paranoid fears and insecurities and showed me how they are wrong. I feel like I can do ANYTHING with his encouragement. I never imagined I would be blessed with such a steadfast best friend.*

We may not have twenty Drakes in our life, but it's so important to have one. Someone who can look at our life—warts, mistakes, challenges, and all—and if there has been subtraction in the past, they switch it over to addition for our future. If this is a season when you've moved away from your "Drake" or you need to find one, look for that person who is a "friend who sticks closer than a brother." Know that even if you're in between such "face-to-face" friends right now, you can have a relationship with Jesus who is such an unshakable, incredible friend. He said, "I will never desert you, nor will I ever abandon you" (Heb. 13:5).

In later chapters, you'll meet people who grew up in difficult situations but who have turned that loss and hurt into motivation for building attachment with their own children. While we know that people reading this can be all over the map when it comes to faith, you'll also see how and why having a strong relationship with our Creator can lift our eyes to real hope. Knowing we are deeply loved can help us make choices for a future different from what we experienced in our past.

Which is one way to say, it's OK if you're reading all this and you find yourself saying about your relationship with your children, "I just didn't know! And so much time has gone by with my children!"

Unless your children are more than 122 years and 164 days old, they *still* desperately need you to love, value, connect with, and seek to build attachment to them. If you're married, your spouse deeply needs you to be that "Drake" in their life as well, and you can learn to do that!

So, let's dig even deeper into how you can begin to *apply* this first element of relational intelligence by answering all three of these crucial attachment questions. These are can't-miss ideas for even normal, imperfect, super-busy homes, like yours.

Three Timeless Answers to Those Three Crucial Questions

You've already heard several times about reaching out and reaching back. Stepping toward or away from. Those "attachment" words have a history, and in one clear case, a timeless one.

Picture a "mega-celebrity" in our day. A Taylor Swift, Drake, Dwayne "The Rock" Johnson, or Gal Gadot level celebrity. Someone you'd expect to have security, a posse, or an entourage surrounding them and making sure the right people come up and the wrong people, like pesky children, keep their appropriate distance.

Then a group of young, excited children do come up. They hope to see this famous person. But they're told by the adults in the room, in no uncertain terms, to get away. And stay away. But the celebrity hears all the commotion. He or she sees what is happening and calls out, "'Allow the children to come to Me; do not forbid them. . . .' And He took them in His arms and began blessing them" (Mark 10:14, 16).

Jesus isn't just a celebrity. But what He did was as countercultural in His day as it is in ours. He came to value people who were too often seen as valueless. Women of the street and corrupt tax collectors, lepers and broken people hiding up in a tree. He didn't walk away from any of them. *But always, Jesus values children.* In fact, He puts one child in His arms and tells His followers that if they want to be "great," then that starts by having the faith of a child. And those weren't just words for His followers.

Jesus sees so much in children that is to be valued. Loved. *Blessed.* And blessing means exactly . . . *what?*

Blessing is a word we believe you need to get to know well. Because while it has timeless and spiritual applications, it's also an amazing tool to apply attachment in your home and right into your child's heart!

To understand how this word, *bless,* can give you three practical ways to apply attachment in your home, let's begin with considering what the word literally means: "to bow the knee." That's a picture of being in the presence of someone of great value. "To bless" also pictures a choice that a parent, grandparent, or loved one makes to add value and love to someone, like offering them life-giving water.

So, when you bless someone, your *attitude* says, "You are very valuable to me," and your *actions* say, "Here, let me add something to your life that you need."

There is, of course, a word that is the *opposite* of blessing. That's to curse someone. Don't think Stephen King and a bloody chicken leg at midnight when you think about a curse. The word *curse* carries with it the picture of "damming up a stream." That doesn't seem so bad if you live in a place surrounded by water. But for desert dwellers like those in the Middle East where Jesus lived, it was a terrible picture. To "dam up the stream" meant that someone who was in a position to allow life-giving water to flow downstream to people and animals who really needed it, instead chose to "curse" those people and subtract life-giving water from them.

Emotionally and tragically, as marriage and family counselors, we see people all the time who have chosen to "step away" and "subtract" anything and everything they can from their spouse. Sadly, when this occurs, children begin missing out on things they desperately need. Things like praise and encouragement. Bright eyes and loving support. Instead, for whatever reason, they "dam up the stream" on whatever could bring emotional and physical life and health.

There is so much more you can learn about blessing people—and getting the blessing yourself (and you can at www.TheBlessing.com). But what we want to look at is how three things you do when you bless a child—like Jesus did—can give you an applied, practical, "I can do that" way of answering those three attachment questions.

Appropriate Meaningful Touch Builds Attachment for a Young Child

Do you remember that first attachment question? *"When you reached out for others, was someone there to reach back?"* When babies reach out, and we reach back and touch their hands or hold them close, that's building attachment. In Bible times, every time a blessing was given to someone, it came with the laying on of hands. Today it can come with an appropriate hug or kiss. As controversial as touch is in our day, it's an absolutely vital aspect of laying down attachment in your home.

Touch is the first way we get to express love to a child in terms a child can understand. It is truly the first language of love. Before babies can even speak a word, they need and react to our appropriate meaningful touch. There are incredible physical benefits when we do reach back to them. Premature babies gain weight 47 percent faster if they're touched and held.[2] Touch lowers blood pressure and helps calm anxiety. When we appropriately touch a child or a loved one, it builds a strong emotional attachment with them as well.[3]

We know, in this #MeToo era, *any* kind of touch seems worrisome and can even seem fearful, not therapeutic or connective. A lot of young parents today struggle with their child going over to a neighbor's house for a sleepover. The Girl Scouts came out with a warning at Thanksgiving to closely watch relatives at family gatherings so that no distant relative or family friend inappropriately (or even just without invitation) hugs or touches a child. Again, that comes from a place of wanting to protect children, which we applaud. But it can also be incredibly confusing or so fear-based that it can result in us withholding *any* touch from a child—including our own!

What we're talking about here is the *need* in a child's life for us to reach back to them with appropriate, meaningful touch. Reaching back to a child who reaches out to us shouldn't be met with fear-based "distance" in our day based on a "hashtag" or cancel culture, any more than it was right for people in Bowlby's day to step back from a hurting child to a "professional distance." When your child is hurting or emotional or tired or happy, touch can be of great value to him or her! That is true for any of us as we grow older too.

An amazing new study on "visual perception" shows how our interpretation of reality can be affected by attachment and touch. Visual perception studies tell us that if *we're alone,* most people will visually measure a hill as being higher and steeper than it is. So imagine a seven-year-old standing alone next to a very high hill.

But now let's say a mom or dad shows up, one this seven-year-old is closely attached to and knows loves him deeply. That person he's attached to stands right next to him, perhaps even holds his hand or puts a hand on his shoulder. Amazingly, with the mere presence of a loved one or strongly connected friend standing near that child, he'll estimate the hill to be *lower* than it actually is, and far less of a challenge to climb than when he viewed it alone! Let's let two scientists explain, in more technical terms, what that means:

Proximity to social resources decreases the cost of climbing both the literal and figurative hills we face, because the brain construes *social* resources as *bioenergetic* resources, much like oxygen or glucose.[4]

In less technical terms, you actually add life and energy, courage and emotional strength to someone when you stand close to that person, when you reach out with appropriate touch or reach back to them when they reach for a hug.

Appropriate touch is an innate need for humans. Just watch the way your three-year-old hugs her "Sugar the blue dinosaur" when she's tired or hurting. How your child responds to your hug when he or she is afraid and runs into your room during a thunderstorm.

We totally agree that it's important to be wise and wary of touch that is inappropriate. Even from relatives. Especially from strangers. But it's not inappropriate for a father to put his hand on his child's shoulder to encourage that child. Or for a mother to give her children a back rub when they're tired. Or to tousle their hair. Or walk back to the car with an arm around their shoulder pad after they lost a big game. Or even do what Jesus did when "important people" around Him told Him to keep those kids away from Him: "And He took them in His arms and began blessing them" (Mark 10:16).

Words Spoken With High Value Build Attachment for a Young Child

A second way to apply attachment and answer those three attachment questions is when, along with our touch, we bless that child with our *spoken* words. We bless when we choose to speak out and say something we see our children have done well or how valuable they are to us. Children need appropriate touch. But they also long for spoken words from the most significant attachment person in their life. *You!*

If you're serious about building attachment, forget the lies found in "Sticks and stones can break my bones, but words will never hurt me." Proverbs 18:21 says, "Death and life are in the power of the tongue." Sound like an exaggeration?

A recent study on *angry words* showed that skin wounds do not heal as quickly in women who are living in a home where angry words are being spoken.[5] And numerous studies are showing that for both women and men who have had a heart attack and survived, if they go back to a marriage where there is severe conflict (think of a place filled with angry words), their likelihood of dying due to a second heart attack spikes dramatically.

Cardiologists and medical experts pushed back on this finding at first. But today, the "life and death" reality that a home with positive, healing, hopeful, loving words can bring health and extend life has energized hospitals to sponsor classes on building stronger attachment.

Notice these are "spoken" words that encourage a child or adult. We have counseled so many people who have struggled with their sense of being attached or blessed by their own parents. A common thing we'll hear from people who grew up without attachment is, "Well, I know I was loved . . . *but I never heard those words.*"

When pressed on this, they'll say something like, "They paid for me to go to college." Or "They came to my graduation from boot camp." Or "They were so busy trying to keep a roof over our heads they didn't have time to say positive words." But if you question them further, you'll hear the deep hurt that, though they may have a diploma, they don't have in their heart words like "I am so proud of you." Or "You are my beloved son or daughter." Or "There are lots of kids out there, but we'd choose you over them all."

The loop does not close on attachment if we don't *say* it.

Parents in those homes are choosing to "dam up the stream" when they don't let life-giving words flow down to a child. That isn't to say they have not loved their child. But they missed out on modeling something incredibly important in a child's life—speaking value to someone. Helping children gain that attachment can, in turn, lead them to explore and love others well.

When we truly love someone, we need to say it *verbally.* Forget all the rationalizations like, "If I say all those positive things, it will just give them a swollen head." Or "They'll quit trying if I praise them and they're already not measuring up to where they need to be." Or "When they grow up, they're not going to hear someone tell them something positive in the real world!" That, unfortunately, is probably true. But it's also the reason that parents are the most important people on the planet who need to use spoken words to bless and say to their children that they do have value!

But what kinds of words really strengthen attachment?

In the next chapter, we'll take a close look at the second element of relational intelligence, *exploration*. We'll go into much more detail on how we can "explore" our children, look at their strengths, and say just what it is that we love and value about them.

Genuine Commitment Builds Attachment for a Young Child

Let's go back to that third attachment question. It's where we are asked if someone not only saw value in us but *did their best to live out a commitment to be there for us.* There will be days when our kids are just hard to bless. Or to even like. Or they will make a mistake. Or they will break our hearts and drop out of school, and we won't see them for three years.

Attachment and blessing call for a parent to do something that isn't easy to do, which is to provide unconditional love and commitment. Again, that is not explaining away bad behavior, but communicating, even in those tough times, that they can count on us to do our best to never leave them nor forsake them.

We've spoken a good deal about building attachment in younger children. But that commitment to be there for a child doesn't "age out." If you have teenagers or college-aged kids, the choices they make can be even more serious and challenging to our commitment to them.

I (John) remember being brought home by the police one time when I was in high school. I'd done something very stupid with a group of friends. My friends were faster, and I was the only one caught. But because this was years ago, and the two local policemen knew my mother, instead of taking me to a holding cell, they took me home at about 3:00 a.m. They beat on the door. Woke up my mother. When she stumbled down the hall and came to the front porch, they reamed me out and left her with a warning that next time I'd indeed go to jail.

We sat down at the kitchen table. I felt so ashamed and sad. This wasn't just something that put you on Santa's bad list. I could have absolutely gone to jail. Which is why, after my mother just sat at the table with me forever without saying a single word (meaning probably a minute or two without her speaking to me), I couldn't take the silence any longer. And I blurted out the words, "Well, I guess this means you don't love me anymore."

I will never forget my mother's head snapping up. Zoa Trent had beautiful blue eyes and dark hair. Her eyes were on fire.

"This has *nothing* to do with me loving you," she said. "I will *always* love you. But I am extremely disappointed in you. This is not who you are. This is not who you will become."

I can remember where we were sitting and what my mother was wearing when she said those words. Words that still saw value in me. Even though I'd made a terrible decision. Words that saw a future for me, even after being brought home in the back of a squad car. She had the commitment to see something inside me and she believed—and because of that, I began to believe—that I was more and could be more than the bad choice I'd made that night.

I knew two things then. First, I was going to be grounded for the majority of my childhood. But I also knew I had someone in my life who was committed to being there for me. Mom showed genuine commitment and was willing to stay attached to me, even though I had just been brought home by the police at 3:00 a.m.

Keep "going to school" on this first element of relational intelligence. It can lay down an unshakable foundation in your child's life. Reach back to your children, see value in them, and stay committed to them. All of these actions give our children the courage to live out for themselves the second element of relational intelligence in children—*exploration*.

IMPORTANT NOTE ON YOUR
"STARTING POINT PLAN" FOR APPLICATION

Here's where you have a choice in building out the "Starting Point Plan" you'll find in chapter 8. Some people learn best by going deeper and focusing on one element at a time. If that's you, then head to chapter 8 and begin building out your plan for this first element. Then go to chapter 4 and the second element.

If you prefer, you can wait until you've gone through all five elements of relational intelligence for children and then work through chapter 8.

Chapter 4

The Second Element of Relational Intelligence: Fearless Exploration

FOCUSING ON FEARLESS EXPLORATION IMPACTS YOUR CHILD'S ABILITY TO:

- *Better understand their limitations*
- *Become an independent thinker responsible for their own learning*
- *Have a healthy curiosity of the unknown before simply barging in*
- *Connect and engage quickly with like-minded people to enhance their own knowledge*
- *Learn to operate from an internal locus of control and be responsible for their response*
- *Become a creative problem solver*

Would you say you're a "pioneer" or a "settler"? Do you feel comfortable with the idea of going out and exploring new trails and opportunities, even heading off down an unmarked or unexplored route? Or are you more of a builder or settler, whose default choice is to do everything you can to limit risk and choose what's known or safe?

As we start our "first day of class" on this second element of relational intelligence, *exploration,* we'll see the optimal way of doing life is being *both*! That doesn't avoid the answer to those questions above on being a "pioneer" or "settler." But you, and your child, can often face a dilemma: Do you reach out and explore? Or do you sit back and observe? And do you have the inner security to do either when it's important to do so?

To be relationally intelligent, we need to have the confidence to begin and continue exploring as long as we can to keep learning and growing. We also need to be wise enough to learn from that exploration! We need to draw on what we've learned in order to make even better choices. That might mean stepping back from some things, but doing so from a position of strength.

If we opt to always take risks for risk's sake (as an example, do an online search of free solo climbing), it can lead to an accident, recklessness, or worse. Winston Churchill, the famed prime minister of England, was a soldier early in his life. After one battle in which he survived a cavalry charge, he famously wrote, "Nothing in life is so exhilarating as to be shot at without result."[1] While that explains why some people take huge risks, there's also one big problem—you could get shot!

Yet if you always take the safe route and are never willing to explore the world around you, that can rob you (and your child) of so much to learn and do in life. Putting safety too high on our priorities can also leave us unwilling to step in to help someone in need because it takes us out of our comfort zone.

Let's kick off our first "class" on this second element of relational intelligence by learning something about exploration from an unexpected source.

The Computer Science of Choosing to Explore

Tom Griffiths is a computational cognitive scientist. He's probably not the first person you'd expect to be good at sharing wise advice on parent/child relationships. Yet Griffiths spends his days trying to figure out why people made wise or foolish decisions and pointing them toward making good ones.

Let's look at something he and other scientists and mathematicians observe quite often when a decision comes up. They call it "the explore/exploit trade-off."

In his wonderful TED talk on "The Computer Science of Human Decision Making," Griffiths shares an example of making a decision on where to go for dinner. Should you go to a restaurant where you haven't been? Or go back to a place you already know has something you like? Here's where the choice to "explore" or "exploit" comes in.

Do you take the risk to "explore" a place you haven't been, gathering in new information that can be of value to you later on? Or do you "exploit" the information you already have, *based on previous trial and error*, and go to a place you already know can give you a nice meal?

Griffiths shares two pictures that are crucial to hold in your mind's eye for a moment. He first puts up a picture of a one-year-old child. This child is doing his very best to put everything he can into his mouth to taste and sample. After all, for a young child, *exploring everything within reach is their job!* But then he puts up a picture of someone old enough to be that child's grandparent. It's a picture of an old man, sitting at the same small table, in the same small restaurant, where he always sits, eating the same sandwich every time he's there. He's exploiting what he already knows about his options and previous experiences.

What's so important about that "explore/exploit" scenario isn't that one is bad and the other is good. For example, exploring is great for a baby. Putting everything in their little mouths is one way infants learn what they like or find delicious or comforting. But that same desire to explore can make us as parents so worried about their getting into our medicine cabinet or putting something disgusting into their mouth!

That grandparent pictured doing the same thing, over and over, already has a wealth of exploration behind him. That doesn't have to be boring. Someone could also say he's making an optimal choice in picking that one sandwich he likes best after a lifetime of making choices. These two mental pictures can point out how you and your child can be at such different stages and places in life.

Your child's job, particularly when young, is to explore. It's part of how children struggle to learn things and narrow down options. For us parents and grandparents, we've been there and done that. We already have the "that's dangerous" or "that's disgusting" T-shirt.

However, if we're not careful we can easily become impatient as our children constantly explore, like wanting to rush ahead and tell them the ending of a story we've already read. Or we can rush in and try to limit any and every kind of risk linked with exploring that might have a negative consequence.

Now, let's acknowledge we're all for wise child safety. Countless articles and books have been written on what to put away to keep a child safe, and for good reason. Prevention is an important way we can demonstrate love to a child.

We know a pediatrician who always ends her appointment with every parent and child she sees by asking the same question: "Until I see you next time, what is your most important job with this child?" And she won't let the parents leave until they say, "To keep her alive."

Yet fear is the natural enemy of exploration and so easy to pick up. After all, we live in an age of twenty-four-hour news cycles. We hear almost every day about product recalls until nothing seems safe to put around our kids. Not cribs or playground equipment. Not even that toy kitchen set you bought at Christmas! There are so many programs like *Forensic Files* and *CSI* on every station, day and night. It doesn't matter if the crime statistics where you live are going up or down. National reporting on child abductions or worse is almost instantaneous today, making it seem like every place in the country is unsafe.

It's easy to become so terrified of what *might* happen to our children that we won't even let them play in their own backyards without us being right next to them. Or let them climb a tree or, heaven forbid, walk the two blocks to school on their own.

We'll talk about "resilience" in the next element of relational intelligence. A key part of what you'll learn is how children's *exploring* can in fact often lead to their falling down. That may mean skinning their knee or even ending up with stitches. But truthfully, *it's only through falling or failing that we learn to get back up*! We don't learn to swim by just reading about it in a book. We have to first face the mental obstacles of swimming and get in the water.

We need to be willing to admit that we're living in a world that can be dangerous and unpredictable. There will always be something to worry about. From the uncertainties of another type of coronavirus to increased gang activity in our city. But we've seen parents whose focus remains on the fear, and whose children will never go to a birthday party or a parade, never travel or go to a camp, never go to a zoo or movie theater, and after the events of 2020, even possibly be required to go to school online and not in a physical building! Each of these presents fewer opportunities for growth and exploration that lead to new relationships and friendships.

It is good to be wise and cautious. But we agree with Kenneth Ginsburg, a Philadelphia pediatrician and author of *Building Resilience in Children and Teens: Giving Kids Roots and Wings*. "Having a child is like having your heart on the outside of your body. The result is that you protect, protect, protect, without realizing that overprotection stifles growth in a big way."[2]

We know homeschool parents who do a great job of making sure their child engages in a co-op or cluster group around science or history lessons. We know public school parents who add on exploration experiences for their children outside of increasingly rare field trips. So be mindful that you are raising a child who is a living, breathing exploration machine. And yes, your #1 job is to keep your children alive. But they gain so much in life by exploring. And *if* they are to become explorers, guess where that begins?

What a "Strange Situation"
Can Teach Us about Exploration

We've seen how we and our children can be at two very different places when it comes to exploration. But let's say we're willing to help them take some risks. To help them explore their world. To love them enough to put them in positions where they get to see more, do more, explore more as they get older. But where does a child's willingness to explore, or the hesitancy to do so, come from?

One answer to this question comes from the work of Mary Ainsworth, a Canadian researcher on attachment in children. A colleague of Bowlby, Ainsworth built on what Bowlby learned by creating something called the "strange situation experiment." Videos still exist of these sessions and can be seen online. They involve mothers and young, preschool-aged children interacting with each other and with others.

The "other" or "stranger" in this case was actually a researcher who would come into the room where a mother and child had been sitting or playing with toys. A short time thereafter, the mother would leave. What would the child do? Remember back to separation anxiety and that primal panic from the last chapter? Inner alarms go off when we're fearful that a primary loved one in our life isn't there and perhaps isn't coming back. And what about this stranger in the room?

While there were several things the child in this study could do when his mother left, the most common was for the child to become initially anxious or distressed. That is healthy and very normal. But then the mother would come back in and the researchers would look at what the child did when she came back. Would the child get angry with her for leaving or go and look for a hug for consolation or reassurance? And then what would happen when the mother left *again*, and what would the child do this time until the mother came back in?

So much was learned in these studies and interactions. But one notable thing for children who were considered "strongly attached" to their mothers was what they did in the room. The children who had a strong attachment to their mother, even if she left and came back, would explore more of the room and play with more of the toys around them. The child would often still be upset when the mother initially left, but would tend to calm down more quickly when she came back in. With the mother now back in the room, the child even warmed up to the stranger in the room.

Which means what?

Although these are controlled experiments, they give a picture of what preschool-aged children do in moving from attachment to exploration. No parent can always be there for their child. There are times when we have to leave the room. But when children know that parent is strongly attached to them, they are also better equipped to trust he or she will come back! They know they can depend on that. They had not been left to do life alone or with a stranger. And when children begin to learn that "She's here for me" or "He's coming back," they feel more freedom to explore what's around them.

We're not saying that you should walk out on your child just to teach them you're coming back. But again, no parents can be there every minute of every day, all during a child's years of growing up. So know that as you continue to build attachment, you're laying the foundation for them to have the courage to set out and explore. You are helping them gain a growing sense of self-regulation regarding their emotions when you do have to step out of the room.

We've seen it's important to realize that our view of exploration and our child's can be very different. We've also seen how attachment indeed lays a foundation for children being willing to take the risk to explore their environment, to reach out to others and to their world. There's another key aspect of exploration we want to focus on as well.

How Doing the Same Small Good Thing Helps Teach Us to Explore

We hope you've seen the movie *A Beautiful Day in the Neighborhood*, starring Tom Hanks, based on the amazing life of Mr. Rogers. When we think of a hero, our minds normally picture someone with a World Series ring or who has earned a medal for valor in combat. But this movie is about a very different kind of hero. A man who spent a very long time helping children of all ages and races do something small that had a big effect on countless children. That was to explore both the happy and sad moments in a child's life.

Some 865 times in 865 television programs Mr. Rogers would walk in, take off that blue blazer, and put on an old blue cardigan zip-up sweater his mother had made. As he put on his comfortable shoes, he'd sing a song about it being "a beautiful day in the neighborhood," and then the *exploring* would begin.

One program they'd explore a happy or even silly feeling. Another time, why we have bad thoughts. It was a children's show, but he would talk with children, in ways they could understand, about the toughest things that children see or hear. From 9/11, to children with physical challenges, to nuclear war, to race relations. He explored in that calm, encouraging, distinctive voice, what was going on inside them.

Mr. Rogers was a "Jedi Knight" as well when it came to exploring what a child thought or felt. Every child he met.

Tom Junod, the investigative reporter whose life story forms the basis of the movie, shares about a time he was with Mr. Rogers. They were in Penn Station where they were taping a television show. After the taping, a long line of children waited to talk with Mr. Rogers. But he was focused on talking with a little boy carrying a big plastic sword.

The mother insisted that the little boy, who watched Mr. Rogers's show every day, give him a hug. But the boy wouldn't do it. He wouldn't even make eye contact with him.

"Oh, my," Rogers said, "that's a big sword you have."

The little boy stared away, saying nothing back. But Mr. Rogers had the patience to stay right there, to keep looking at, seeing, and exploring this little boy. Then he leaned over and whispered something in the boy's ear. Something that made the boy lean back, finally look at Mr. Rogers, and nod his little head. Here's how Junod captured what happened:

We were heading back to his apartment in a taxi when I asked him what he had said.

"Oh, I just knew that whenever you see a little boy carrying something like that, it means that he wants to show people that he's strong on the outside. I just wanted to let him know that he was strong on the inside, too. And so that's what I told him. I said, 'Do you know that you're strong on the inside, too?' Maybe it was something he needed to hear."[3]

We wish there was a way to bottle that kind of patience, focus, love, grace, and exploration that Fred Rogers reflected. He was truly one of a kind. But we can learn from him to not just explore what's on the outside of children, but what's at the core of what they're thinking and feeling as well.

For example, we don't just look at the deed our child has done—like throwing a fit at the grocery store. Instead we slow down to see the "need behind the deed," maybe noting that it was 10 p.m. when we took him to the store with us because we got off work so late. He's worn out, hungry, and tired. And now throwing a fit.

When our friend Dr. Tony Wheeler, a family counselor and coach, speaks to parents attending a seminar, we've heard him often say, "It's easy for us parents to get so busy, we wake up one day and we've missed a *decade* in our child's life. *A decade where we never really saw them.*"

We can and should keep taking the risk to explore our world and encourage our children to do likewise. But as parents, we also need to explore our children. To look at them. Listen to them. Ask questions of them. It builds attachment into our children's lives, so even when they're in that "strange situation," they're gaining the confidence to keep exploring their world.

It is especially important, in our super busy lives, to work at exploring and trying to understand what our children are feeling—even when we've had a tough day. To not be dismissive of their fears. To not minimize their goals. We can get down on their level and take time to play and listen and pray with them when we put them to bed. Before we wake up and a decade has gone by and we don't really know them.

We're just scratching the surface on why exploration is so important. There's much more you can learn at therelationallyintelligentchild.com. But let's dig into how you can *apply* this need for exploration, both in encouraging your child to be an explorer—and also in exploring your child.

Tools for Applying
"Fearless Exploration" in Your Home

Exploring for Very Young Children

Young children are fascinated by how things work. What things look like inside. How they are made. Using all their senses, including taste, touch, and smell is normal. Normal is climbing. Playing with water. Opening cabinets. Getting into purses. Touching anything within reach. They approach dogs, cats, people, often without evaluation or fear—at least initially. Exploring everything as a toddler leads to playing with everything—which is their work in mastering new mental, physical, and social skills.

So encourage little ones to explore and keep opening up new play places. Let them clean up after a bath or help you with chores, helping you do the dishes or sweep. Understand that when they're old enough to do chores well, they don't actually want to do them. But when they're too young to do chores well, they love helping out! Studies show that children who are allowed to help early on are actually much more willing helpers later. So let them jump in and help you with the dishes. (Have some towels nearby.) Or let them take over pushing a broom for you and watch them do it over and over as they try to master the skill. Be fine with early explorers doing tasks imperfectly.

Know that nature is tremendous exploration territory. That doesn't require you taking a four-hour car trek to the forest. Just take your children for a walk around the block or to a small local park and let them explore. And realize as well that children have different attention spans at different ages when it comes to exploring. It's okay if they switch to exploring something else.

Exploration as Your Child Gets Older
20 Questions

Macaulay Culkin was the ten-year-old star of what has become the highest-grossing Christmas movie of all time, making more than $285.7 million since it was first released. But in the outstanding Netflix series *The Movies That Made Us* we find out the reason he got that starring role in *Home Alone*. It was because of one scene in an earlier movie Macaulay did with John Candy, called *Uncle Buck*.

It's the scene where Culkin walks into the kitchen and meets his uncle Buck for the first time. *"Who are you?"* he says, staggering back, with that wide-eyed innocent look. But then he sits down and starts asking his uncle Buck rapid-fire questions.

We counted twelve questions in a row he asks his uncle Buck in a little more than a minute. "Where are you from? Are you married? Do you have kids? Why not? . . ." Finally, John Candy asks, "What's your record for consecutive questions?" And without batting an eye, he answers, "Thirty-eight!"

Any parent who has watched that movie can relate. Most children go through a stage in life when they are question-asking machines. "Why can I see myself in a mirror?" "Why do some flowers have stickers?" "Why do we have to cook cookies?" "Why" is a powerful way they explore their world.

But what we may not realize as parents is that a key to building relationally intelligent children is our asking questions back. It's a great way to explore our children and encourage their curiosity!

I (John) played a game with my kids and their friends that became something of a family legend. It came to be called "Twenty Questions." It started on a day I was tasked with picking up Kari, our older daughter. I'd been told we'd be bringing home a new friend (who became her best friend) named Bryne from school.

After I endured the wait in the car-pick-up lane, the two of them finally piled in. That's when I noticed a tennis ball in my cup holder. Not based on the movie, but with similar results, I told the girls that on the way home, we were going to play a game called "Twenty Questions."

I would ask, and they had to answer twenty questions before we got home. That meant I would hand one of them the tennis ball and then ask her a question. She would answer and then hand it back. Then it was the other girl's turn.

"How was your day?" I asked, handing Kari the ball.

"Fine," she said, handing the ball back.

"How was *your* day?" handing the ball to Bryne.

"Fine." Bryne handed it back from the backseat.

I eventually got better at asking more open-ended questions. They eventually got warmed up and started actually answering with more than one-word answers. Then we hit some topics that took even longer to answer. Before we knew it, we had been parked in front of Bryne's house passing the ball back and forth until her mother came out to see why she wasn't coming in! Answering twenty questions provided us a very fun and informative conversation.

That game went on for four years every time I picked them up, until they started taking the bus to junior high. It became a modeling of "exploration"—and became something they'd do with different friends we'd take home. Now it was them saying, "We're going to play a game called 'Twenty Questions' . . ."

It's so important that we learn how to explore our children. To ask questions. To express an interest. Be patient. Know that at first they'll likely be limited to only one-word answers. Keep at it though. It's amazing how patience and just one question, after a long list of short answers, can open a door to something important they're thinking or feeling.

Your child isn't the only person in your life whom you need to be passing that ball back and forth with. We both do a great deal of marriage counseling. Almost without exception, the couples we see who are in trouble have quit exploring each other.

When couples are in a healthy relationship, they'll explore each other's thoughts. Ask about what the person is thinking. Share about their dreams and perhaps even their fears. But conflicted couples tend to learn what not to talk about. As soon as it becomes an emotional discussion, or too time consuming to really listen, the other person turns away.

One key way to apply this second element of relational attachment—exploration—is with positive, probing questions. It doesn't have to be twenty questions—or thirty-eight. No tennis balls are required. Only a willingness to ask and then listen to their answers. Then ask for clarification. Then another question on what *they think* they ought to do about that situation. In doing so, you'll start getting to some of those heart issues.

Mr. Rogers It

We shared earlier how Mr. Rogers was world-class at exploring people. Based on that, here's an application skill you can implement, which we'll call "Mr. Rogers It."

If you've seen even one episode of *Mr. Rogers' Neighborhood*, you'll marvel at the running commentary he engages in with children. It's an amazing picture of what "exploring in real time" looks like, and it encourages a child to keep working and exploring.

You can do this with your child. For example, with your three-year-old, *when you "see" it, say it.* As you're watching your child play, explore what the child is doing by saying what you're seeing. "I can see you're really working hard to get all those rings on the post. It's not easy getting that last one on, is it?"

Or with a seven-year-old, "I'm noticing you are really concentrating on those math problems. Walk me through what you're doing there."

There's a reason sportscasters "call" a game that everyone can see. It gets us engaged! Particularly with younger children, *saying what you're seeing* helps them feel like they are being explored. And your exploring what they're doing, or struggling with, can keep them exploring.

Never Waste an Errand in Exploring Your Child

My (John's) mother struggled mightily with rheumatoid arthritis. That may have been the incentive for her to take us boys along with her to the store to help her lift or carry things. But for her, the world was a classroom, and every trip offered a lesson in exploring the world in front of us, which gave her a chance to explore us. From the moment we got in the car, she began asking questions and making observations that modeled active learning for us as kids.

Whatever we saw and commented on, Mom noticed and asked us questions about, whether it was driving by a construction site or passing a stalled car or noticing a blooming tree. Just being alert to what was around us offered natural opportunities to explore how things were built, the need for maintenance, and the way seasons work.

It takes longer to do a run to the home-repair shop when part of what you're doing is exploring with your child. You don't have to point out everything in the store or on the way there and back that might be an opportunity for exploration. But do recognize there are so many opportunities. "If you could go home and make anything you want, what would it be?" "You really like those big trucks on the construction site, don't you? Is that something you could see yourself doing when you grow up?"

Use Technology to Open Doors of Exploration

We're all for you cutting back on technology use where you can. But there are still ways to use technology to bring exploration into your child's life.

For example, let's say you're on vacation, and you're planning a trip to that city's natural history museum. You might download the museum's app, but then have your kids grab paper and crayons and create their own written "map" of the things they want to see while you're there. And after your visit, ask each child to talk about one thing he or she learned or saw that blew their mind. What were they amazed by, and why?

Or if they are studying volcanos, look up some appropriate YouTube videos to bring more life to what they are learning. You can use technology as an active-learning *asset* instead of a passive *pacifier*.

Start a "Free Range Kids Club" or Take Them to a Family Camp

Much of what our children do today is incredibly structured due to safety concerns. But some parents, including some parent groups, are defying that social norm and putting their children in less structured settings, encouraging them to explore what's around them.

What has prompted this movement of parents today in many cases are men and women who remember having much more freedom and far less fear in their days growing up. For example, in grade school, being allowed to visit a neighbor's house without an adult going with them. Even perhaps going down to the local store. While I wouldn't recommend it today, I (John) was told almost every summer day, "Go outside and don't come home until the streetlights are on!"

One such group of parents wanting more "open range parenting" for their children can be found in Chicago. Parents who remember having much more freedom in their past. Yes, parents in the city, not a suburb of Chicago. The same city that has been struggling mightily with gun violence.

In a wonderful special report in the *Chicago Tribune*,[4] Lisa Pevtzow followed around a group of young children, mostly fourth graders. Once a week, they meet up and wander around their neighborhood on Chicago's North Side—unsupervised.

They call themselves the "free range kids" and yes, they've been coached and have a group of supportive parents encouraging them. It's led by forty-year-old Monica. She was one of those who, as a child, had the freedom to run around and wants that for her children today. So she organized a group of parents who wanted the same thing for their children.

They began by laying out ground rules and safety rules. The kids have cellphones and know what to say to an adult who asks where their parents are. Or what to do if someone says something that makes them feel uncomfortable or unsafe, which thankfully hadn't happened when the article was written. What had happened was the children reporting that on their own, they now knew how to walk around their block without getting lost. How to order lunch by themselves at a nearby diner. How to safely cross the street.

If putting together a "free range" group where you live seems too far outside your comfort zone, then here's a suggestion we (the Trent family) did for twenty summers in a row. Go as a family to "exploration heaven" for your child at an outstanding family camp.

For us, this began with going to a noted family camp called Pine Cove in the beautiful woods near Tyler, Texas. A family camp has meetings for the parents and age-graded experiences for the kids. But there is also plenty of free time each day.

After our first year at camp when our kids had learned the ropes, and every year thereafter, during free time our kids would take off by themselves and run to find a group of friends. They'd spend several hours each day, within the boundaries of this huge camp, doing fun things together. From hiking to canoeing, from fishing to skipping rocks. They explored free time to roam all over the camp without an adult two feet away from them.

Both our girls have often commented on how much that made them feel like they were growing up. Taking responsibility for themselves. Learning to explore on their own—but in a safe environment. Yes, there are risks even in Tyler, Texas. Or on the North Side of Chicago. But part of a parent being willing to be relationally intelligent is looking for ways to let your children experience freedom as they learn to explore.

A Page-Turning Way to Help Them Explore Their World

We've stressed safety and the importance of minimizing hazards, particularly for younger children, as well as embracing exploration in healthy ways. But something else has inspired millions of children, and grown-ups, to go out and explore. And that's to put a book in their hand.

Even if they're reading a book on their iPad, anything you can do to put an adventure story in front of children can open their eyes and minds to exploration. Introduce them to great heroes, fearless explorers, champions who stepped up to help hurting people. So many people can inspire them through the pages of a book.

A good thing to do can be to take your children to a library. Find the children's section and locate books about people like Ben Franklin, Harriet Tubman, or Neil Armstrong. Then after reading about them, have your children talk about what they learned. So many inspiring stories can help a child get the picture that while exploring can be challenging, it pushes us forward in life and helps us learn new things. It gets us inspired to help or step toward people who are hurting. Reading opens doors to adventures and places we'd like to explore.

So you've been "going to school" on two elements of relational intelligence. Giving our children the loving *attachment* they need is so foundational for all the rest. *Fearless exploration* gets your child moving and reaching out and keeps us exploring our child's interests and dreams, hurts and fears as well.

But as we're about to see, as in learning to walk, there are times when our children will fall down. The goal isn't to make sure they never fall, but to help them know how to get back up. That is what we'll dig into with the third element of relational intelligence for children: how to help your child live out another key word, *resilience.*

IMPORTANT NOTE ON YOUR
"STARTING POINT PLAN" FOR APPLICATION

Remember, you have a choice in building out your "starting point plan" you'll find in chapter 8. If it's helpful and the way you learn best, then head to chapter 8 now and begin building out your plan for this second element.

Or you can wait until you've gone through all five elements of relational intelligence for children and then launch your "starting point plan" in chapter 8.

Chapter 5

The Third Element of Relational Intelligence: Unwavering Resilience

Child Abuse or Building Strength?

Resilience is one of those words almost all of us seem to like. It suggests having determination, stamina, and the strength to overcome adversity. Until COVID-19, for most of us this word likely brought to mind a time in our country's history like World War II or even the Great Depression. Today, all of us living have now gone through an unprecedented, nationwide "war" against a virus with even greater than Depression-era effects.

We've all had to learn lessons in patience and resilience. Parents are more aware than ever that our world can change dramatically quite quickly. Our children need resilience perhaps more than ever before. But it's also safe to say not all parents go about building resilient children the same way—or do so at all, for that matter.

For example, helicopter parents and snowplow parents have been scrutinized and blamed in recent years for failing to firmly establish healthy levels of resilience in their children. On the other end of the continuum, others practically see as abuse how some parents go about instilling resilience.

Considering some of the increasingly popular parenting styles today, we are forced to wonder, "Just how resilient are our children?" It depends on who you ask. According to a resilience assessment report published in 2019 by Everyday Health in partnership with Ohio State University, many Americans appear to *overestimate* their personal resilience. They found that 83 percent of Americans surveyed believed they possessed high levels of emotional and mental resilience. Yet the data revealed only 57 percent actually scored as resilient. The study certainly has relevance today because 60 percent of those surveyed were millennials and Gen Z. More specifically, of the 3,583 participants ages thirteen to seventy-three, 1,324 were millennials (ages twenty-three to thirty-eight) and 823 were Gen Z (ages thirteen to twenty-two).[1]

Before we take a deeper look at resilience through additional research, let's establish a logical definition for resilience that can serve as our lens moving forward.

Resilience Defined

Resilience can be defined clinically as "the ability to successfully adapt to stressful situations and recover from difficult challenges." For those serious about raising resilient children, we say it's the ability to fall down and get back up on one's own.

Who among us doesn't want to deal in a healthy way with stress and anxiety? Having resilience is important; some experts believe it is even essential for success in life.

Dean M. Becker, one of the founders of the resilience training firm Adaptiv Learning Systems, stated in a 2002 *Harvard Business Review* article that "More than education, more than experience, more than training, a person's level of resilience will determine who succeeds and who fails."[2]

Being resilient is proven to have other benefits as well. Individuals who demonstrate higher levels of resilience tend to be more optimistic. They also are able to greatly reduce the negative emotions that keep people from bouncing back from adversity, meaning being able to filter unnecessary negative information when evaluating bad news. Not that it doesn't hurt. Or break their heart. They don't minimize the reality of a situation, but they are able to put to one side that challenge, or in some cases defeat, and instead pick up strategic coping skills to take that first step, and then another, in facing adversity.[3]

The Everyday Health Special Report also shows resilient people are able to keep their challenges in perspective by not overanalyzing or allowing small things to derail their efforts, whereas less resilient people tend to spend excessive amounts of time cycling through the loss or engaging in negative self-talk. They may regularly say things to themselves like "What a loser" or "I'll never figure it out." Or use more passive, defeated attitudes such as "Whatever!" or "It is what it is" or "It doesn't matter."

Please note, that isn't the same thing as saying or feeling those things once or even having them pop into our minds every once in a while. However, Martin Luther is attributed with saying, "You can't keep birds from flying over your head. But you can keep them from building a nest in your hair."

It's normal for a child, or a parent, to feel discouraged. To feel down. To grieve a loss. To be confused and ask "Why?" As we'll see, discouraging times are great opportunities to sit and listen, not always having to find a solution or try to minimize their pain. But remember that characteristic of resilience. It's that inner reminder that it's raining now, but someday—even in Seattle after thirty straight days of rain— the sun will come out. Optimism and the first step toward "getting up" are linked to a resilient heart.

In the same report, among low levels of resilience, where negative self-talk goes on and on and people move toward long-term discouragement or significant anxiety, researchers reported a more widespread presence of medical and emotionally damaging conditions. Links to asthma, diabetes, chronic stress, and eating disorders are found among individuals scoring low in resilience.[4]

Let's look at the origins of this third element of relational intelligence—or why it can fail to launch in our child's life.

The Messages We Send Our Children

Children today are easily exposed to vast amounts of negative and inappropriate information, which has led many parents to implement drastic measures to protect, or oftentimes overprotect, their children. Although many of these measures are warranted, the following still seems worth considering: a lot of the things that have potential to harm us can also help us become more resilient.

Ask yourself this question: When you face challenges or experience a defeat in life, do you have a "fixed" or "open" mindset? With all the *potentially* harmful things around us, we can have a "fixed" mindset, meaning, no matter what, we are committed to do all we can to not expose ourselves, or our children, to any possible hurt or loss. If that's our default setting in the reality of challenges, it can go a long way toward our children failing to learn to face normal, day-to-day responsibilities. They may find it hard to cope with even the smallest of challenges.

Does that sound like a "fringe" position toward parenting and childhood? It's actually become far too close to the norm.

In 2016, a school located on one of the Channel Islands between France and England cancelled a beach trip. The reason? Fear of the students' exposure to too much sunshine.[5] The possible message to a child: I'd better stay away from the beach because sunshine can hurt me!

We've just gone through a period when nearly everything was shut down for fear of a virus. But we've also seen parks and schoolyard playgrounds being closed to children across the country due to incorrect or insufficient protective covering on playground equipment or court surfaces. The possible message: I can't be trusted to remain safe on my own or test on my own if something is too hot or unsafe.

A teacher in Florida was fired for giving zeroes to students who failed to turn in their assignments instead of the 50 that was mandated by school officials.[6] The possible message: I'm entitled to at least half-credit for not completing (or not even starting) a task. Or, for students who did their work, why should I work so hard when people doing nothing receive almost the same as me?

Many college administrators are being required to strongly evaluate what and how things are communicated on campuses in order to avoid the risk of causing discomfort or offending students with opposing views. A number of colleges have created safe places for students experiencing high levels of anxiety and depression resulting from their inability to cope with normal responsibilities associated with attending college.

We realize this is coming very close to raging controversies in our country today. For some people, saying the words "That triggered me!" is a way of escaping any negative thought or discussion. You as a parent will certainly decide the level of challenge you allow your child to face. But the absence of having to deal with any real-life problems and challenges doesn't create resilience.

For example, more teenagers today are opting for alternative means of travel instead of driving themselves. Not necessarily for convenience sake, but more so because they prefer someone else taking on the risks or challenges associated with driving.

In a world that seeks shelter from almost any challenge, we are asking you to consider what expectations and entitlements your children might be developing that could lead to them being less resilient as adults.

What if we could teach our children more about dealing with issues instead of running away from them? There are a legion of challenges they can't outsource to avoid, find safety from, or pretend don't exist.

We wish we could say this is an optional element of relational intelligence. But it's right at the heart of what a child needs to learn to relate wisely and well with others.

We've seen the innate and important element of exploration necessary for children to learn and grow. But there is that real-life possibility that when they reach out or explore their world, someone might not reach back or they might fall. So let's dig into what helps them get up and keep moving toward a positive future.

Characteristics of a Resilient Child

In thousands of hours working with hundreds of parents, we've identified clear characteristics of resilient children, developed over the course of childhood to young adulthood. It's helpful to know that just as our children are wired for attachment and relationships, they are wired to be resilient.

For example, exposure to various allergens can make us uncomfortable, but they also can help your child to build a stronger immune system. Physical resilience also explains why skin naturally forms a scab and heals after we scrape our knee or elbow. When children first begin to walk, you don't have to tell them to get back up when they fall. Even though parental encouragement can lift their spirits, most children eventually get up and learn to walk! And children have a "flight or fight" system wired in, keeping them safe if they are scared by a barking dog.[7]

Along with their God-given wiring to be resilient, they can have a strong, foundational attachment with you, giving them the courage and confidence they need to fearlessly explore their world. Here, then, is that resilience list.

Resilient Children Know How to Interact with People Different from Themselves

Frankly, because making friends and dealing well with people different from us can be hard for us, we can limit or assume our children need to step away from others. The chairman of our Strong Marriages board of directors is named Eric. He and his wife, Caroline, have three precious daughters, ages six, four, and almost one, and are some of the wisest millennial parents I (Dewey) have met.

Eric and Caroline are very intentional about teaching their daughters how to interact with people different from them. They believe it's important for their children to not only be exposed to people outside of their immediate world, but also learn to graciously accept and serve people who aren't as fortunate as they are. Eric and Caroline would certainly never put their children in any danger, so they are always right beside them, guiding them in what to say and do. When one of the girls struggles to interact with different people, Eric typically sets her down and gently reasons with her. Eric and Caroline know the more their children learn to effectively interact with others as children, the more successful they will be as adults interacting with people at work and other community environments. In the end, they learn by Mom and Dad's example, which happens to be a huge commonality in every characteristic we'll discuss.

Encourage your children to lead the way. As you learned in chapter 4, children who experience a secure attachment with their parents are also typically better at connecting with other people. So taking advantage of opportunities to bond with your children is a great place to start. Encourage them to make the first move when interacting with people who are different. School events, birthday parties, or sporting venues are great places to practice learning these skills. When you lead the way and participate with them, they are more likely to engage themselves.

Afterward, like Dr. Trent did with Kari and her friend, ask open-ended questions in order to learn what they thought about their experience. Ask questions that will draw out any feelings of discomfort they may have experienced. But be sure to highlight the bright spots and celebrate the positives. Helping your child have relationships with peers, their teachers, grandparents, trusted neighbors, and those on their sports teams teaches them the importance of developing healthy networks of friends. A model of engaging with others can provide support and encouragement all their lives. It also teaches them to value, respect, and empathize with people who don't think the same as them, which is something *so* needed today!

Resilient Children Tend to Be Confident, Creative Thinkers

I (Dewey) remember our granddaughter, Kimber, getting her first pair of really cool rain boots when she was around three years old. She couldn't wait to show them off to Gramma and PawPaw, so she brought them along on a sleepover at our house even though there wasn't a cloud in the sky. The following morning, she burst into our bedroom after waking up super early, ready to go play outside. Her shirt was on backward, and her jeans were tucked into her rain boots, which also happened to be on the wrong feet. After celebrating her attempt at getting dressed herself, we helped her correct her wardrobe, then made our way to the backyard to play together in the imaginary rain.

Events like this are a pretty good indication your child is cognitively processing through information before making a decision that seems logical. Kimber processed through what she remembered about getting dressed. What she apparently forgot, couldn't comprehend, or simply wasn't taught was which boot went on which foot and that her clothes were designed not to be worn inside out. These children tend to exhibit higher levels of self-confidence and self-esteem. They also tend to be self-thinkers who make logical decisions, and that's even when they don't agree with friends or other people. Another benefit to helping your children be autonomous is they learn to operate from an internal locus of control as adults. Although that sounds like a big clinical phrase, it simply means they believe their decisions and behaviors affect the outcome of life events opposed to an external locus of control, which is a person believing environmental circumstances beyond their control causes their responses to be what they are.

Allow your child to be independent at home. Starting at home is a great way to teach your children skills like getting dressed, brushing teeth, and bathing while also allowing them to make mistakes in the process. At mealtime, encourage them to do things like help set the table or pour their own drink even though the chances are greater they could spill it on the floor or counter. Encouraging your children to take risks under your supervision helps them learn healthy boundaries and self-regulation. Give your children responsibilities around the house. Giving them a list of chores to complete and letting them finish them in the order they choose teaches them planning skills and gives them opportunities to celebrate achievement. Remember, teaching your children by engaging alongside them, modeling what you want them to accomplish, helps them perform skills without expecting others to do things for them later in life. Lastly, by modeling self-discipline and taking responsibility for your own journey in the face of adversity, you help instill confidence and courage in your child to do the same.

Resilient Children Ask for Help from Others They Trust

You might be wondering what asking for help from others has to do with becoming resilient. Actually, a lot. Recently, I (Dewey) was counseling a young couple in their twenties having major problems learning to effectively communicate with each other. Each time we began an exercise, the husband would have a very difficult time staying engaged, even though the tasks I assigned him were relatively simple to complete. Within minutes, he would generally become very frustrated, push his papers aside, and let us know what we were doing was stupid and senseless. After the dust settled a bit, I asked him the following two questions: (1) Who took time to teach and support him the most growing up? (2) Was he given opportunities to ask for help when things were difficult?

I wasn't surprised when he looked away and answered the first question, *"No one."* He told me his dad was seldom around after his parents divorced and his mom worked two jobs to pay the bills. So no one was around for him to ask for help. He assertively told me he was left to figure things out on his own. Like his mom, he learned resilience by working hard and providing for his family, but because he was left alone so often as a child, he never learned to ask for help in accomplishing certain things after they became challenging; therefore he quit.

Help your children discover options. Children who struggle with asking for help quickly become frustrated or overwhelmed to the point they sometimes feel completely hopeless. If you are experiencing any of this behavior from your child, help your child understand frustration is a natural emotion that can notify the child it's time to consider slowing down or stopping the process altogether. Challenge your children to think of other options or methods for accomplishing the task. After helping them decide what option is best, give them time to test their procedure. Should their attempts fail again, share with them that it is perfectly acceptable for them to ask for help. Only don't stop there. Teach them how and when to ask using respectful words and tones. Some examples might be:

- I have tried (the following options) and nothing has seemed to work. Could you help me understand why and possibly help me do it?
- Is this a good time for me to ask you a question regarding _____?

Helping your children learn acceptable options for pushing through challenges by first attempting what they know, and if necessary reaching out for help, will make it easier for them to succeed in every relationship as an adult. It sends a message to others that they aren't perfect, they don't have all the answers, and they value other people for who they are and what they know.

Resilient Children Are Able to Accept "No" as a Sensible Answer

Growing up, my brother and I (Dewey) gave our parents many opportunities to use that small yet powerful word *no*. Today, I believe it was probably the most sensible response at the time, but I'm fairly certain I didn't think so when it happened. For example, why are there toy aisles in grocery stores? Saturday was grocery shopping day in our family. Almost every time we walked through the door, I headed right to the toy aisle, already knowing my mom would yell out, "No touching! And, no, you're not buying anything to take home!" You know, I really don't think we ever did.

A lot of parents today quickly succumb to their child's requests after initially answering no, especially when the no is answered by whining, crying, or screaming. Frankly, these are very natural responses for small children because that's what they do as babies when they are hungry, tired, sick, or need their bottom cleaned. Teaching your children to accept no without acting like a baby can be challenging, but being successful now will greatly decrease the likelihood of them throwing fits as adults or racking up tons of debt because they fail to accept why it makes sense to say no in the moment.

Nine Steps for learning to accept "no." Children, no matter their age, have the capacity for learning how to accept no for an answer. Older children that have seldom been told no may have a more difficult time grasping this concept, but the steps to follow are basically the same.

- Listen closely to your child's request. Children will ask for things when they know you're busy (e.g., when dinner is being prepared). Older children tend to manipulate your answer by knowing when to ask.

- Determine whether the request is valid. Sometimes you think you know what your children are asking before they finish asking. Listen first, then evaluate.

- If no is the answer, wait for the child's response. If they don't completely blow up, consider offering a suitable option. For example, instead of giving them a cola before dinner, offer them a no-sugar, no-caffeine drink.

- If they accept, commend their decision and celebrate their behavior.

- If they completely blow up, your response is critical. Walking away should definitely be considered as you don't have to apologize, or explain for that matter, what you don't say when angry. Remember, you're the adult.

- Help them understand that by blowing up they lost the option to at least get out of bed and get something to drink, which typically is just another stall tactic. Instead, they must remain in the bed, while you get them the drink. Gentle reasoning after the dust settles can be very effective. People, regardless of their age, seldom learn new principles in the midst of a crisis.

- Stick to your decision. Caving in to any bad behavior simply because you're tired of dealing with it or possibly embarrassed when it occurs in public will only make things worse next time you tell them no to the same or similar request.

- Don't allow family and friends to offset your progress. Emphasize and even overemphasize the importance of having their support, even if they don't agree. You might have to consider certain boundaries should they not be willing to partner with you.

- Remember: the more consistent you are, the more consistent your children become.

Resilient Children Finish What They Start

Commitment and perseverance seem to be two words missing from a lot of kids' vocabulary today. We believe one reason is that as parents we don't want our children to fail, be uncomfortable, or be rejected, so we tend to swoop in and finish or fix things for them. In fact, yesterday's helicopter parents are today's snowplow parents. Instead of hovering over children and landing to rescue them when things become too difficult, these parents simply plow a path for their children so they don't have to face certain adversities. Instead of not finishing what they start, they never have to finish what the parents started for them!

Have you ever noticed that quitting can be a lot like cancer? When quitting is allowed once, it becomes easier to quit something again, then quit something else, then another thing . . . and before you know it, quitting has become such a natural response it spreads into every aspect of life. Not to sound fatalistic, but a habit of quitting that's unchecked in childhood, often turns into failed marriages or walking off numerous jobs in adulthood. Really! Helping your children stay committed and persevere through the smallest things will help them be more resilient in big ways later in life.

Ensure the task aligns with their capabilities and skillset. Our five-year-old granddaughter loves to complete puzzles. Allowing her to start a two-thousand-piece puzzle and demanding she stick with it until the last piece is totally unrealistic. But requiring her to finish a fifty-piece puzzle that she chose to start is certainly logical. Requiring her to persevere with patience even when it's difficult builds commitment.

Allow adequate time for your child to start and finish. Not giving your children time to successfully complete tasks sends them mixed signals. We would often tell our daughter, Erin, to stop what she was doing and put her things away as we were about to walk out the door. Then we would get upset at her when we noticed a lot of her things were crammed into her closet. Once we realized it was unfair to require what we didn't allow time to do, Erin became much more orderly with her things.

Do your research and know everything that's involved and expected. Just because something looks like it ought to be simple doesn't mean it is. Setting up your child to succeed means you're going to have to do research to learn exactly what it is your child will be doing. Then, once you decide, be clear in sharing everything involved with the activities your child wants to start. For example, things like level of difficulty and duration.

Make sure your expectations are realistic and communicated clearly. Constantly moving the goalposts causes confusion, frustration, and eventually failure. We realize you're super busy and must multitask almost every minute of every day. But how sensible or logical is it for you to hold others accountable for what you don't take time to clearly communicate?

Don't allow your child to get involved in too many activities at once. If we're being honest, almost all of us are guilty of violating this principle. It was a sad day when my wife, Lynne, recommended our younger daughter, Erin, stop playing girls' fast-pitch at the age of nine. She was a natural at playing catcher to some really good pitchers who were older than she was. But she was also a natural at dancing and performing. So, knowing she really loved dancing, I reluctantly agreed. A few years later, when her dancing and singing started to interfere with her schoolwork, we had to decide which activity had to go. Realizing she could possibly receive a college scholarship with singing, we had to say no to her dancing. Although she didn't like the decision at the time, it didn't seem to matter as a high school senior when she received a phone call letting her know she would be attending college on a singing scholarship. As a parenting team, or seeking wise counsel from others if you're a single parent, identify what seems to be natural or come easily to your children. Also consider whether or not they pursue it with passion, continue to excel, if it can possibly provide a path for college and career, and if it consistently brings them joy.

Clearly communicate that not finishing what they start is unacceptable. There are times when quitting is acceptable, like with an unexpected move or physical injury. But enforcing your child's need to complete a season in sports or an activity in school teaches commitment and perseverance. When quitting is allowed just because something is uncomfortable or difficult, the next decision to quit happens more quickly and easily, oftentimes without considering any possible consequences. Keep this in mind when allowing your children to begin new activities.

Be a good example. Demonstrating healthy balance and perseverance is essential to your child's success. We believe the term *crisis* can be defined in the following way: "A crisis becomes a crisis only when a person's ability to manage the situation or circumstance in a rational manner becomes expended." In other words, how a person copes with adversity and challenges often determines whether the outcome is a victory or a defeat. Because you are reading this book, you probably have a good feel for what's going on among your children today. By creating a secure attachment with your children, you're giving them permission to safely yet fearlessly explore their world, which means they will face adversity. But by developing your children's ability to successfully bounce back from those adversities, and helping them effectively manage future challenges, you are basically teaching them how to roll over, float, and breathe more freely in a pool that wants to bring them under.

At six years old, our granddaughter swims like a fish. After many years of swimming lessons with her instructor and guide, she is able to safely hold her breath while swimming down six feet to retrieve the pool dart on the bottom of the pool. Her training continues in order for her to reach her goal of learning to scuba dive by the age of ten.

We have more to guide you through as well if we're to successfully help you reach the goal of you and your children becoming more relationally intelligent! So turn the page and let's discover how what you just learned about resilience is the platform for helping your child make wise personal decisions.

IMPORTANT NOTE ON YOUR
"STARTING POINT PLAN" FOR APPLICATION

Remember, you have a choice in building out your "starting point plan" you'll find in chapter 8. If it's helpful and the way you learn best, then head to chapter 8 now and begin building out your plan for this third element.

Or you can wait until you've gone through all five elements of relational intelligence for children and then launch your "starting point plan" in chapter 8.

Chapter 6

The Fourth Element of Relational Intelligence: Wise Decision-Making

FOCUSING ON WISE DECISION-MAKING IMPACTS YOUR CHILD'S ABILITY TO:

- *Not make decisions based solely on emotions*
- *Understand that while feelings are real, they're not always reliable*
- *Value experiences and insights learned from others*
- *Initiate a decision, opposed to always waiting for someone else to decide*
- *Effectively weigh both the positives and negatives before making a decision*

There were always two sides to having a brother two years older than me (Dewey). The positive side was being able to learn from his mistakes and always having someone to protect me from the monster I believed was living under the bed. Later on, it was great when he, as a senior in high school, protected me from other seniors who wanted to haze me as a sophomore.

The negative side was getting his hand-me-downs and often having him make me do things when we were young that I knew would get us in trouble.

Every summer, my brother and I got to spend two weeks at our grandmother's house ... without parents. Having raised two children of our own, I can only imagine what it felt like for our parents to get a break from us for two weeks. But for us, once they dropped us off and headed back home, we knew we were in for two action-packed weeks of fun, getting to do pretty much whatever we wanted. Most importantly, it meant being free to explore my grandmother's private community completely unsupervised.

Our ability to explore got even better the summer our parents allowed us to take my *used* minibike and my brother's *new* motorcycle they had given us a few months earlier. I was only allowed to ride the minibike, because, at the age of eight, my parents must have thought I couldn't handle anything faster. I disagreed with their assessment that my brother was somehow so much more mature at the age of ten and, therefore, qualified to ride a bona fide motorcycle when I wasn't. One morning shortly after we arrived, my brother, along with our cousin who had joined us on the trip, came up with the harebrained idea to steal a piece of concrete yard art from a house a few blocks away. I was never given a choice to decline, but instead was designated the lookout guy who would park down the street and whistle if someone showed up during the caper.

Fortunately, no one spoiled the plan and we pulled off the heist unscathed—*or so it seemed*. In the process of getting away, my brother and cousin, with stolen yard art in hand, flew right past me a lot faster than I knew my minibike would be able to go. As they disappeared over the horizon, I began to panic with visions of me wearing a striped prison suit at the age of eight. What made it worse was I figured I would be the only one busted for a robbery they planned! Knowing I needed more speed, the only thing that came to mind was trying to get more out of the throttle located on the right handlebar by grabbing it with both hands. I immediately knew that was an unwise decision. The moment I did it, the front wheel turned hard to the right, and I went airborne over the front wheel. Thankfully, God protected me because no bones were broken nor was my head cracked open from not wearing a helmet (looking back, this was, unarguably, the most unwise decision of all). I still have the scars more than fifty years later as reminders of God's protection and just how foolish our decisions were that day.

It goes without saying that the best antidote to making unwise decisions is learning to make wise decisions, right? I mean it sounds reasonable, but can it really be that simple? In fact, some parents seem to take the position that children are simply going to make bad decisions, so they should just expect them to take risks and try foolish stunts. Some scientific research even seems to support this line of thinking, concluding the majority of teenagers are psychosocially immature, so parents can expect them to make impulsive decisions, struggle with delaying gratification, fail to anticipate consequences, and engage in risky behavior because of the excitement such actions offer.[1] Neuroscience has discovered certain information about the child brain that helps provide further explanation for why this phenomenon occurs.

According to Deborah Yurgelun-Todd, a neuroscientist at Harvard's brain imaging center, the brain region responsible for upper-level reasoning and decision-making doesn't fully mature until an individual is in his or her early twenties.[2] Other research shows that functional changes happen at a slower rate in the part of the brain that evaluates and determines consequences than in the area of the brain that seeks and prompts rewards. That basically means that for adolescents, illogical, unrealistic rewards outweigh any logical consequences due to underdeveloped areas in their brains. What's more, the gap seems to widen when the activity occurs in the presence of peers.[3] Maybe this explains why my brother, my cousin, and I were simply doing what young boys do. No harm, no foul, right?

We can think of some good reasons why parents shouldn't simply accept statements like those without first considering what's at stake. The Bible tells us that "Even a child is known by his deeds, whether what he does is pure and right" (Prov. 20:11 NKJV), thus making the child accountable to God and others. But here is another good reason: *the decisions made by your children will most likely determine the direction of their lives as adults*. Helping your children effectively make and manage decisions wisely when the stakes are fairly low decreases the likelihood of them making unwise decisions that could possibly have catastrophic consequences later in life.

While my minibike accident could have been much worse, I'm grateful for parents who quickly used our unwise decision-making as learning experiences while we were young. In addition to our returning the stolen yard art, it took many months for me to work off the doctor bill and the minibike repair bill. However, that gave me ample time to think about my bad decisions as well as rehearse in my mind the physical pain I endured and the mental pain I caused for people who love me. But frankly, we boys weren't the only ones responsible for making unwise decisions. Our parents made a few as well. For example, they obviously didn't consider what was at stake by allowing me at eight years old to get on a minibike without protective head gear. In addition, there's a good chance I wouldn't have left so much skin on the pavement had I been wearing something with more skin coverage than shorts and a T-shirt. The fact is, every parent also makes unwise decisions from time to time.

What we are about to share regarding wise decision-making will be presented a lot like how we introduced and discussed the content in each of the three previous chapters. We'll first provide you with a good working definition for both unwise and wise decision making. Next, we'll examine a practical approach to help you better understand the cognitive process of how both you and your children tend to make decisions. Having a good understanding and mental concept of this process will make it much simpler for you to (1) relate well and connect with each of the applicational steps, and (2) put them into action more quickly. Let's get started by defining wise decision-making.

Defining Wise and Unwise Decision-Making

Hoping to find a suitable definition for decision-making, we discovered many definitions were simply too long and detailed for our purposes here. We created a more clear, comprehensive definition we thought would better apply to our discussions in this chapter. Therefore, we propose:

- **Wise** decision-making is a mental process wherein the individual first considers the risks involved and any possible consequences before taking action.

- **Unwise** decision-making is a mental process wherein the individual is willing to take action before considering the risks involved or any possible consequences.

Did you know every single decision we make has an outcome or effect? That's hard to imagine, especially considering each of us makes thousands of decisions every day. Some of those decisions occur quickly and automatically, while others happen more slowly and intentionally. For example, say your "hunger notification" goes off in your stomach because you haven't eaten in hours. You automatically decide it's time to eat. The outcome? You decide to go out to eat, and now have to decide where to go, which will also have an effect on what you eat. After arriving and looking at the menu, you're not sure what you want to eat. So, before you can ever reach your final outcome of satisfying your hunger, you must now engage in a slower, more intentional decision-making process. Many brain experts call this intentional process "cognitive decision-making," which involves the following seven steps:

1. *Identifying the decision.* This is the moment you realize a decision needs to be made (hunger notification). This is a very important step, because how accurately you pinpoint the type of decision to be made will greatly impact the following steps.

2. *Collect relevant information.* This means gathering resources that are applicable to the circumstance. Some resources will be obtained internally (e.g., What am I hungry for? Where should I go? Did I like what I ate the last time I went there?), and other resources externally (e.g., searching online, on a phone app, or calling a friend).

3. *Consider possible alternatives.* Processing through relevant data typically reveals possible alternatives (e.g., locations with best atmosphere, or better fries, or I can order something special).

4. *Weigh the information.* Does the information gathered meet the perceived need, and will it lead to favorable emotions? (e.g., After eating _____ at _____, will I be full, satisfied, and happy?)

5. *Make a choice among the alternatives.* After weighing all the information gathered, you're ready to choose based on what you've determined best suits you (e.g., I'm going to _____ for a burger, fries, and soda).

6. *Put decision in motion.* Time to take action and put your plan in motion.

7. *Evaluate your decision along with outcomes or consequences.* Did your action successfully resolve your need or desire? At times, you will probably need to repeat certain steps in order to obtain better results or simply decide to move ahead.

Whew! It sure seems like intentional decision-making expends a lot of cognitive energy. You might be thinking, *Having to go through this process for every decision will only leave me feeling mentally and emotionally spent!* But actually, the way we're able to make thousands and thousands of decisions each day demonstrates the complete awesomeness of God. And, even though neuroscientists are still making new and exciting discoveries, what we already know for certain is our brains were designed by God with the capacity to store magnificent amounts of information in our long-term memory, along with the inexplicable ability to access, evaluate, recall, and assign information at unimaginable speeds. Apparently, God already knew that we and our children were going to face certain situations where we are required to slowly process through the decision steps already mentioned, and other times when we will process through the steps so quickly that our decisions and responses occur automatically and subconsciously. Through discoveries in recent years, neuroscientists now offer a very logical explanation for this phenomenon called neuroplasticity that all parents today should know.

In addition to long-term memory, each of us also has what is referred to as working memory. Some of the main functions of working memory are to control our attention, temporarily hold smaller units of information like phone numbers and instructions, and help guide decisions and carry out plans.[4] However, unlike long-term memory, working memory has a limited capacity in how much information it can effectively hold before becoming overloaded. That amount is plus or minus seven, meaning the brain can only hold somewhere between five and nine different units of data at one time, and can organize and compare no more than two to four elements at any one time.[5] Thankfully, also by God's design, almost all of the decisions we make daily have been made so many times they have become automatic and have very little taxing effect on our cognitive abilities.

Yet here is something parents today need to consider. Most of the information needed to effectively make wise decisions is stored in long-term memory almost like files in a filing cabinet. This information is only useful when it is identified and retrieved back into working memory before being applied to the decision-making process in each unique situation. If there happens to be too much going on in working memory at the time specific units of information should be retrieved, those units become bottle-necked like traffic in a traffic jam. Therefore, it is increasingly more difficult to make wise decisions. Even though millennials and Gen Zers are considered by many to be the ultimate multitaskers, the facts concerning working memory haven't changed. When our children are doing multiple things at once, like wearing headphones, listening to music, playing games on the computer, checking TikTok or Twitter, and texting their friends all at the same time, it becomes next to impossible for them to effectively process information needed to make wise decisions.

Unfortunately, the working memories of our children are too often absorbed with so much noise that it's incredibly difficult for them to recognize what's going on all around them that they're missing. Another thing that is extremely difficult when children max out their cognitive capacity is their ability to be more creative. Less cluttered working memories also increase the capacity for original and creative thinking. You may be thinking your child simply doesn't have creative or critical-thinking abilities, when instead the issue is they're trying to cope with an excessive mental load. In fact, research demonstrates the mind naturally produces innovative thoughts when not under severe cognitive mental load, instead of defaulting to only familiar associations like many psychologists have assumed.[6] Apparently, there's much to be said for minimizing the amount of cognitive load brought on by interfacing with multiple digital devices and social media.

When the number of units held at one time in working memory stays well below these amounts, it is much easier for individuals to not only effectively make quick decisions but also have the ability to slow things down in order to explore new options that could lead to making new wise decisions. This is the reasoning behind one popular theory today involving exploiting or exploring memory for making decisions that we mentioned in the chapter on exploration.

Exploiting occurs more rapidly because it is the process of using only familiar and available information for making decisions. Using the eating illustration we did earlier, choosing a familiar location to eat and ordering the same thing each time is a good example of exploiting units of information in long-term memory in order to make a quick decision. It requires less time and cognitive energy. Taking time to research a new location and then taking additional time to browse the menu before ordering is a good example of exploring new units of information before making a decision. This explains why we seldom choose someplace new and different to eat when we are in a hurry or have too many things going on at once.

As you can see, there's a lot more to making wise decisions than the average person probably realizes. And, while what you just read is really more like taking a forty-thousand-foot view of how our brains process information and develop emotions holistically, hopefully you now have a better perspective of how and why you and your children tend to make decisions and why it's so important to avoid cognitive overload in the process. Now, over the next few pages, we're going to guide you through some proven wise decision-making recommendations and application steps guaranteed to help your child become more self-regulating in this area. Remember, it's incredibly important that you not only use these application steps in developing your plan, but also work through these steps with your child if your plan is going to be successful.

Self-Regulation

I (Dewey) love taking my five-year-old granddaughter, Kimber, to breakfast almost every week. In addition to hanging out with PawPaw, she knows we're going to the fast food restaurant that includes a toy with children's meals. As we walked through the door one morning, we were welcomed by a young lad around three years old on the floor screaming and giving us his best impression of a breakdancer. The child's mom, appearing unaffected by her son's behavior, told us the meal that was supposed to make him happy didn't include the toy he wanted, so he was sharing his unhappiness with the rest of us. As she quickly scooped him up to go find a table, Kimber and I ordered pancakes with extra syrup, even though I was supposed to be on a diet watching my calorie intake.

The young boy falling out on the floor and me giving in to the temptation of pancakes with extra syrup both look a lot like a lack of self-control. But actually, they are both good examples of poor self-regulation. Self-control is about restraining strong, unhealthy desires, and self-regulation is what makes self-control possible. For the child, self-regulation would be having the ability to avoid major outbursts by keeping his emotions in check despite being confronted with the undesirable information he received from his mom. It's learning to modify expectations and successfully handling frustrations that would otherwise lead to bad behavior. Self-regulation for me as the adult is behaving in a manner consistent with deeply held values and long-term goals in the face of temptation or despite strong opposing thoughts or feelings. It's sticking with a diet for the sake of reaching a long-term goal of losing weight. Or it could possibly be someone getting up and going to work in order to get a paycheck even though rolling over and getting more sleep would feel better.

Self-regulation doesn't happen naturally, yet it's one of your child's "must haves" in order to create and operate within specific limitations. Limitations become protective barriers, along with the moral and ethical compass needed to guide them through building relationships and dealing with unexpected circumstances that most assuredly await them later in life. But here's something for you to consider. Your children can develop self-regulation skills by proactively learning how to make wise decisions before the need arises. They can develop self-regulation by experiencing consequences associated with unwise decisions in a safe environment with people who love them deeply. Otherwise, they will struggle to self-regulate while suffering the repercussions of consistently making unwise decisions in a "me first" world full of uncaring people. Just by your reading this book, we know which you prefer for your child! So let's look together at a few recommendations we have for teaching your child wise decision-making.

Recommendations for Making Wise Decisions

We realize not all of the following recommendations will apply to your children. That will likely be determined by their age and what they are currently experiencing in their particular environment. However, we are asking you to keep an open-growth mindset as you consider how any or all of these could possibly apply to your child. Remember that learning to make wise decisions does not occur overnight. Once your plan is developed and implemented, it may take many weeks for your children to change their behavior. Stay the course, and your hard work and perseverance will be rewarded.

Model Wise Decision Making

There were times when my parents' response to my bad decision wasn't open for discussion. However, I never remember hearing either one of them say, "Do what I say, not what I do!" In our society today, there are plenty of opportunities for your children to be exposed to hypocrisy without accountability among authority figures. The last place they need to see such behavior is in their home. You shouldn't expect your children to do what you say when you refuse to set a positive example, but you can expect to have a much better chance of them following your lead when you do.

Application Steps

- Be intentional to model making wise decisions both in and away from your home. Most of us are more conscientious to avoid gossip or openly discrediting others when we know people are watching and listening, even when the observers are people we've never met. We also tend to model good behavior when the consequences are obvious, such as losing our job for wasting time on the internet rather than efficiently completing the tasks we are financially compensated to perform. Be mindful of how you act toward or speak about others in front of your children at home, including talking about someone you're watching on TV. Also, if you don't want your children watching inappropriate movies later, set the standard for them while they are living under your roof when there is a greater likelihood of them learning from your actions. Instead of bragging about getting more change back from your server in the restaurant or grocery store after you and your children leave the building, allow them to watch you return the money, even if it means getting out of your car or returning to the store after making it back home. When you mess up, take time to apologize and discuss your unwise decision with your children. Lastly, it's never too late to start.

How it helps your child become self-regulating

When you set a high standard and model wise decision-making, your child learns the value of making ethical and moral decisions and is more likely to make them later in life.

Set Clear Boundaries

Relational boundaries are generally intangible parameters that delineate between what is safe and acceptable, and those things that cause conflict and can potentially harm others. Setting clear boundaries for your children helps them: (1) realize there are specific benchmarks in life that provide them a point of reference, and (2) know when, how, and how far to push before stepping beyond the boundaries and experiencing the consequences of their behavior. Trying to hold your children responsible for what they don't know doesn't work. But communicating clear boundaries will result in your children taking responsibility for their decisions and their actions.

Application Steps

- Set age-specific boundaries. Don't expect your children to operate within unrealistic boundaries. For example, don't expect your three-year-old to act responsibly with your iPad. Be sensible by only allowing your children to interact with age-appropriate digital devices and responsibilities. Your boundaries may also change as they grow and mature.

• Intentionally communicate what you expect. You can't expect what you don't express. While unavoidable at times, setting boundaries on the fly will eventually be viewed as constantly moving the goalpost. Having meaningful conversations about your expectations provides them with a mental checklist and demonstrates commitment and partnership to your children.

• Allow them time to act. By not hovering over them or constantly watching them with the eye of a hawk, you enable them to become autonomous in their decision-making. We're not advocating you just turn them loose, but be sensible in allowing them to operate within your boundaries.

How it helps your child become self-regulating

As your children hear you communicating clear boundaries, they begin creating mental representations of what is considered to be acceptable behavior. This process alone is critical for solidifying data in your child's long-term memory, which is generally used at a later time to determine acceptable limitations.

Be Mindful of Giving Clear Consequences or Making Clear Ultimatums

Children need to know there are consequences to making unwise decisions, but should they know the exact consequences each and every time? I (Dewey) recently had a good friend tell me he and his wife had adopted a new parenting philosophy that has revolutionized decision-making with his girls. They call it "fuzzy ultimatums," meaning they no longer give clear ultimatums for violating boundaries. Like many other parents, they learned their four- and six-year-old girls would mentally evaluate whether the "clear" consequences were worth the risky, selfish behavior. They discovered on occasions it was! Once the parents opted for not giving clear consequences for their ultimatums, their girls started asking what would happen should they violate a clear boundary. He told me the success rate of their girls now staying within boundaries had skyrocketed after implementing this new strategy.

Obviously, there are times when children should unequivocally have clear consequences for making unwise decisions that lead to risky or bad behavior. But even as a parent, you would likely agree there are times when you mentally weigh possible consequences before acting; therefore, we should expect our children to do the same from time to time. While this philosophy may not be suitable for every parent, children who are uncertain about consequences for unwise decisions will be less prone to act out.

Application Steps

- When not giving clear ultimatums, take time to ask your children what they are thinking. Ask them to verbalize what they believe are possible consequences. However, if your plan is for them to not know exact consequences, be careful not to give away your plans in your response or even with your countenance.

- Follow through with your plan. Children can be persuasive, so stick to your strategic plan for disciplining your children through consequences. Remember, being inconsistent sends confusing signals, which typically leads to additional unwise decisions.

How it helps your child become self-regulating

Maximizing options always requires intentional thinking, and at times even creative thinking. The process of your child considering possible consequences often requires them to creatively expand their knowledge base. Additionally, experiencing some of those same consequences helps them learn to control their emotions and successfully manage difficult circumstances in the future. Remember, you can't expect what you don't inspect.

Actively Participate in Their Decision-Making Process

Apart from your children learning to make wise decisions as you model the behavior you desire, children also tend to learn wise decision-making through your actively teaching them deductive reasoning. Deductive reasoning is processing through available data in order to reach the most logical or suitable conclusion. We recommend you consider following these steps:

Application Steps

- With smaller children, consider setting out two or more sets of clothes each morning before asking them to choose between options. Require them to only choose between available options should they not like any of your choices. After the choice is made, ask why they chose what they did. You will likely need to guide the conversation the first few times. Repeat this exercise at bedtime by asking them to choose a book or story to read. Keep asking follow-up questions as long as they are participating.

- Use fictitious characters (dolls or stuffed animals work great) to help them see why some decisions are important. For example, should your child not want to take a bath, go to bed, clean their room, etc., ask them what they think would happen if _____ never took a bath, went to sleep, cleaned their room, etc.? Guide them in the direction you want them to go.

- The same exercise can be done with older children with themselves as the subjects instead of fictitious characters. For example, ask them what might occur if they miss their ride home or find themselves in an unlawful situation such as amidst peers doing drugs. Help them develop a plan for removing themselves from the threatening situation. Ask questions like, "What would you tell a friend should they be in a similar situation?" Remind them the importance of asking for help.

- Help your children with managing schedules and calendars. Scheduled events will often overlap each other. Helping your children make wise choices with their calendar now helps them stay balanced later. Intentionally ask questions about upcoming events.

How it helps your child become self-regulating

Children will not learn how to cope with a crisis while in the middle of a crisis. Actively participating in creating and acting out scenarios and what-if exercises are proactive methods for helping your children deal with challenging or undesirable situations in the future.

Allow Your Children to Experience Consequences without Rescuing Them

Sometimes the most difficult thing as a parent is being on the sidelines while your children experience the burden of consequences after making unwise decisions. Like adults, children learn and implement needed change best when they (1) have enough knowledge that they want to, (2) have enough resources that they are able to, or (3) have enough discomfort they are required to. It would be great if our children only needed to be told once when learning to make wise decisions, but we know that is illogical and unreasonable. That said, like with all other children, there will be times when the best possible way for them to learn the value of making a wise decision is for them to experience the consequences of making an unwise decision. But guess what? *Suffering takes on a whole new perspective once one has meaning and understanding.* The key is your children knowing you are there, and you knowing when to engage.

Application Steps

- When you are responsible for administering consequences, be intentional in your actions. At times, a cooling-off period can be good for your children to think about their actions. It can also be the time they need to get to a place where they can reason through their consequences. Even so, consequences often need to be swift and certainly experienced in the time frame they are told.

- Establish and communicate healthy ground rules for experiencing consequences. Children experiencing the proper consequences associated with making bad decisions can be extremely helpful for them and less emotional for you. Clearly communicate what is going to take place. Remind them to carefully choose their words, or that continued bad behavior comes with additional consequences.

- Allow natural consequences to run their course. For example, allow your children to experience the consequences associated with losing their favorite stuffed animal after leaving it in the basket at the grocery store. Obviously, you will need to decide the amount of effort you put forth in returning to the store to see if the animal is still there. Not immediately replacing the animal teaches the child to consider the actions that led up to the crisis event. The same process can apply to teenagers leaving backpacks or even consistently and carelessly forgetting a cellphone.

- Part of the consequential process is helping them process everything that took place. Take time to communicate with your children, asking things like, "What would you do different next time?" Children seldom respond well to condemning or criticizing, so think carefully before asking questions or making comments about their behavior.

- Consequences are both bad and good. Teach your children this truth by celebrating when they make wise decisions!

It's not to say you praise them each time they perform normal responsibilities like getting dressed or brushing their teeth. Although it is good to occasionally acknowledge those events, when your child receives a good grade after studying hard for weeks, celebrate it with something special. Be sure to ask them questions like, "What emotions did you feel after working so hard and getting the grade you hoped for?"

- Keep your emotions in check. Parents often take two steps backward or lose premier teaching opportunities by losing their cool or saying things they later regret. Take the appropriate amount of time to process through your emotions before administering consequences. Should they resurface, remember you never have to apologize for things you don't say. Excuse yourself and put some time and space between you and what seems to be triggering your strong emotions.

How it helps your child become self-regulating

Remember that good self-regulating skills enable self-control. Experiencing consequences together with someone they know loves them when the costs involved are relatively low can be the best possible self-regulating training for your children. Muscles don't get stronger without experiencing the pain associated with sensible exercise. In the same way, our children get stronger through adversity and experiencing sensible consequences under your supervision. Lastly, we seldom forget what we learn through our experiences. Maybe that's why God uses our physical scars as visible reminders—*so we won't forget!*

The Wisdom in Having Read
This Far in This Chapter and Book

Throughout all of our years of counseling families, we have seen very few people who weren't striving for autonomy and independence while also wanting desperately to be loved and accepted for who they are. Interestingly, so many of these family members were never trained to be independent, wise decision-makers as children. In addition, many of these same people tend to view most of their life consequences as unfair or unwarranted. Most of them never learned to value the refining and teaching benefits that can come with experiencing sensible consequences of unwise decisions earlier in life.

We are incredibly proud of you for taking the time to read this book. We are honored to guide you as you learn everything involved with these first four elements of relational intelligence. Hopefully you have been frequently checking out the blogs and additional information we have for you by visiting our website at therelationallyintelligentchild.com. Now, let's see how each of these elements of relational intelligence can prepare you and your children for service—to God and to others.

IMPORTANT NOTE ON YOUR "STARTING POINT PLAN" FOR APPLICATION

Remember, you have a choice in building out your "starting point plan" you'll find in chapter 8. If it's helpful and the way you learn best, then head to chapter 8 now and begin building out your plan for this fourth element.

Or you can wait until you've gone through all five elements of relational intelligence for children and then launch your "starting point plan" in chapter 8.

Chapter 7

The Fifth Element of Relational Intelligence: Future-Focused Service

FOCUSING ON FUTURE-FOCUSED SERVICE IMPACTS YOUR CHILD'S ABILITY TO:

- *Develop "altruistic" attitudes*
- *Quickly identify ways to make others' situations better*
- *Seek sustainable, long-term solutions that benefit others and not just temporary fixes*
- *Sacrifice their own needs for the needs of others when necessary (like helping a hurting child or calling out bullying)*
- *Be forward-looking, living life with purpose and meaning*

(Dewey) have always loved watching my wife, Lynne, create cakes for special occasions. In fact, I think she could hold her own competing against the professional bakers who create those incredible cakes on TV. I remember one instance years ago, when the alluring aroma of a freshly baked cake led me into our kitchen where she had just removed three rectangular cakes from the oven.

Totally consumed with curiosity, I asked, "What are you making?" She replied, "Winnie the Pooh sitting up and holding a jar of honey." With that vision in mind, I looked back at the three rectangular cakes on the counter and replied something like, "It'll be great!" even though in my mind I'm sure I was thinking something more like, *I have to see this to believe it!*

I should have never discounted her abilities, because when I entered the kitchen a few hours later, there on the counter sat a lifelike replica of a brown Pooh Bear about sixteen inches tall holding a small golden yellow jug of honey. The detailed character likeness was impeccable. But what impressed me the most was how she took three cakes baked in rectangular molds and somehow transformed them into something so entirely different than what they were originally. Looking totally astonished, I asked how she ever pulled it off. Using her famous "It's no big deal" look, she replied, "Once you have it in your head, the rest just sort of happens."

Think back for a moment to chapter 1. If you remember, I told the story about my doctoral dissertation and how easy I thought it would be to prove the hypothesis that narcissistic millennials would struggle with commitment to long-term relationships. Already being labeled narcissistic by society, the "me first" attitude of millennials would naturally portray a lack of commitment. But that wasn't the case. Instead, when surveyed, only a very small number of millennials across the country scored high enough to be considered narcissistic. But how could that be when their generational status had already been determined?

Kira Newman, content writer for Greater Good Science Center in California, published an online article titled "The Surprisingly

Boring Truth about Millennials and Narcissism."[1] In her tagline she says, "We've stereotyped the younger generation as self-absorbed—but behind the headlines lies a nuanced scientific debate," a debate she expounds on concerning whether millennials in general, and/or the Generation Zers that follow them, truly are narcissistic, and therefore warranting their being stereotyped as self-centered, entitled, lazy, and unrealistic dreamers. (For more information regarding Kira Newman's article, visit www.therelationallyintelligentchild.com)

Let's consider for a moment that members from these two cohorts possibly do possess an elevated sense of entitlement and strive for greater individualism and autonomy. However, that's not because of narcissistic personalities in general, but it's driven instead by personality characteristics and mindsets developed from being overly coddled and protected, excessively praised, and given awards for simply showing up. We're not implying these young adults and children today are without responsibility. But could their predecessors labeling the entire two generational groups narcissistic possibly help diminish the sting of reality that these relatively rapid changes occurred on their predecessors' watch?

You see, stereotyping or assigning labels creates a psychological mold made for individuals. Unfortunately, this opens a door for people outside the mold to make fundamental attribution errors about the behavior of the people in the mold. For example, let's say after placing a coffee order, a young adult or teenager stands frozen in front of the counter clicking on her phone. The older adult behind her in line becomes frustrated and assumes the self-centered, narcissistic millennial is probably posting on Facebook and cares only about herself, but instead it's because she just received notice her apartment was burglarized.

Stereotyping makes it easier for people to attribute the behavior of the stereotyped person to poor character and not consider possible alternatives.

Considering alternatives means we must spend time in face-to-face communication getting to know the class of people we are stereotyping.

Another interesting factor found in Kira Newman's article that was consistent with some of our research is the phenomenon known as "stereotype threat," which means "stereotypes become self-fulfilling prophecies because people are worried about confirming them." In other words, it's similar to Lynne's response that once she has the vision of the cake in her head, the rest just sort of happens. It can become easier to believe something about yourself after hearing it over and over to the point it eventually becomes engrained into your thought patterns, causing your behavior to just sort of happen. It's a fact that whatever we believe about any aspect of life will be reflected in our behavior in that area of life.

So, if you are a young parent who's bought into stereotypes of your generation, take notice and be hopeful! Do your best to stop defining yourself by general attitudes of a self-gratifying culture and comparing yourself with other people's presentations of themselves on social media.

Instead, start comparing yourself today with the version of yourself yesterday.

Based on personal experiences and a myriad of research completed in recent years, instead of stereotypical narcissistic millennials and Generation Zers, we see some of the most incredibly gifted and talented individuals who have the potential to impact their future in unique ways not seen before. Unarguably, dynamic changes in technology dictate future growth of society, and let's face it, no other generation understands dynamic technology as well as millennials and Generation Z.

The majority of young people have a passion and desire to make a positive difference in their culture today. Despite what is often reported about millennials and Generation Z, the majority of them are well-educated team players who believe strongly in their future.[2]

Research also indicates young adults are engaged in philanthropic endeavors. Varying data suggests not all millennials are actively engaged in volunteer work,[3] but the majority we interact with are! Additional studies suggest that in order for millennial and Generation Z cohorts to make significant positive impacts in their future, more collective action for their common good is needed.[4]

Before taking a look at some incredible application stories about people engaged in future-focused service to others in home, community, country, and world, let's talk about altruism for a moment. Altruistic service to others is future-focused and purposefully driven by a disinterest in self or a selfless concern and true compassion for the people being served. Simply stated, it is service with a purpose, opposed to helping others in order to benefit self.

It's so easy to have the mindset that "it's our world and everyone else lives in it" mindset. Confusing as is. As humans, we are prone to start each day by thinking about ourselves. Just to test that theory, do you remember your first thought this morning when you woke up? Most likely, you took a personal evaluation of how you felt physically, or about the first thing you needed to do in order to get something else done!

In one of Martin Luther King Jr.'s final sermons, given two months before he died, he talked about greatness: "If you want to be important—wonderful. If you want to be recognized—wonderful. . . . everybody can be great . . . because everybody can serve."[5] If you are a millennial or Generation Z parent, you likely don't need to be persuaded to become altruistic, because many of you take pride in already being idealistic and altruistic. (For more information about altruism and altruistic behavior, visit www.therelationallyintelligentchild.com.) Who among us doesn't have aspirations of being great at something? Well, here's something for you to think about.

We are all created by God for doing life together in relationships with each other. It's His idea. It's His plan. He designed it, and He knows the best way for us to live it out. We thrive best, both individually and collectively, in future-focused service to others; therefore that should be one of our primary goals in life!

So, here's some of the most exciting news we can share. After learning the previous four elements and beginning to live them out in your life while simultaneously teaching them to your children, engaging in future-focused service will be the natural output of your efforts.

We've seen how, in many ways, this fifth element of being relationally intelligent is a capstone to the other four. It's right at the center of what millennial and Gen Z parents are awesomely prepared for and want to do. Let's look, then, at how we can model and help our children learn those skills that we've learned for doing life and point them toward positive, *future-focused service* for others. We could be frozen in fear at the challenges in our world. Or fatalistic that life will never get better than it "used to be" in times past. But we are convinced we and our children were made for a purpose—and for a "special future." That includes us learning and living out service, starting right in our own homes.

Future-Focused Service *in Your Home*

The best starting place for lifting your child's eyes to see and serve others is right in your own home! That can begin with something as simple as engaging them in doing chores that aren't being done to benefit your house—but those who live in it.

We know most children love to do chores with us when they're really too young to do them. And when they're old enough to do chores on their own, they don't want to do them. But helping others shouldn't overlook those in our home.

As you link your children with chores, keep several things in mind. First, realize that children move at a different pace than most adults when it comes to *completing* tasks. Particularly young children. If you're on the more "driven" side of things and committed to getting chores done fast, know that that can frustrate a child who isn't looking as far forward as you, and instead is doing life more in the here-and-now of childhood. "Come on! Speed up! The game's coming up so let's get this done!" may not leave the best memory of connection and purpose in finishing a chore.

In addition to chores around the house, lift their eyes to incredible sources of love that need caring for—their pets! If your child is raising a snake, this won't work as well. But if your family has an average, lovable, crazy dog or an affectionate cat, let the children jump in on helping feed them and keeping their water bowl full. Get them involved in brushing their pets and throwing them a ball or taking them for a walk.

Talk to them and praise them for stepping in and helping. But whatever "acts of service" you invite your child to do to meet needs in your home, strongly consider giving your child an "official" title when you do.

In a recent study at the University of California–San Diego, researchers found that if they used a noun ("Will you be a *helper*?") opposed to a verb ("Will you *help*?"), 22 percent more children jumped in to help. That isn't just a psychological trick to get them to help you get something done. Instead, it can help them get a picture of who they can be. Who they want to be. Christopher Bryan, lead researcher on the study, writes of his study, "This research suggests that preschool-aged children are already thinking on some level about the kind of person they are, and are taking on an active role in shaping that identity."[6]

"I appreciate you being a helper" is a great way to praise them. And after they get started helping out at home, the next step is to raise their eyes to serving a need in their neighborhood.

Future-Focused Service *in Your Neighborhood*

Nicholas Lowinger was only five years old when he visited a homeless shelter with his parents that wasn't too far from his home. While he was there, he met a brother and sister who were homeless. It shocked him when he discovered they were taking turns going to school. That's because they only had one pair of shoes between them and had to take turns wearing them.

Nicholas gave the boy a pair of basketball sneakers, which certainly helped that family. But it also launched Nicholas, with his parents' encouragement, on a quest to try to figure out ways to help more children in other shelters. Today, through an organization he founded to help the homeless called Gotta Have Sole, more than 99,000 children in homeless shelters have shoes who didn't before.

Most likely, there's someplace close, perhaps right in your neighborhood, where you can take your children to help them see people with real needs, who aren't "somewhere else" in the world.

For example, the couples class that we (John and Cindy) led for many years went as families to a local retirement home one Christmas. We encouraged the children to bring an instrument if they played one, or to practice a piece that they could play on the piano there. Other children were encouraged to bring a favorite book or game to share with a newly made elderly friend. Almost twenty families fanned out and talked with, laughed, encouraged, sang to, played games with, and blessed a number of elderly residents. It was Christmas Day, which required a sacrifice from every family to take part of their day to go help a neighbor. But had these families not chosen to be there, the vast majority of those residents wouldn't have had a single visitor or been able to meet new friends that Christmas Day.

Not every visit to help out in a local church's thrift store or nursery, or serving food at a soup kitchen, will result in your child starting a national outreach. But it can be a powerful way to open their eyes to the needs of others, not just in your home, but also in local neighborhoods as well.

Future-Focused Service *for Your Country*

Alexandra Scott, who was lovingly called "Alex," was born in Connecticut in 1996. Tragically, she was diagnosed with neuroblastoma, a type of childhood cancer, shortly before she turned one year old. In 2000, just after turning four years old, she informed her mother she wanted to start a lemonade stand to raise money for doctors to "help other kids like they helped me."

Alex's first lemonade stand amazingly raised two thousand dollars. But she wasn't done. Inspired by that first stand, Alex, with her parents' help, created Alex's Lemonade Stand Foundation. Alex continued her lemonade stands throughout her life, ultimately raising more than one million dollars toward cancer research.

Alex fought hard, but she died in August 2004 at the age of eight. Since her death, Alex's Lemonade Stand Foundation has sponsored a national fundraising weekend every June called "Lemonade Days." On that single day each June, as many as ten thousand volunteers serve in more than two thousand Alex's Lemonade Stands around the nation, remembering her life story and the difference made in so many sick children's lives all over America.

Stories like this lift our eyes to the amazing things a child's heart to serve can do. Instead of despairing that her future was unsure and simply giving up, Alex set aside her own hurts and looked toward finding cures to help children like her, children who would come after her.

Small things, like one lemonade stand, can do big things. So too can putting your children in a position to be grateful for what they have in their country, as well as thankful for the chance to serve those in other countries.

Without realizing what would happen in the life of our girls, I (John) remember being asked to do two back-to-back "retreats" one summer. The first week, we all gladly left the heat of Arizona and went up to a five-star dude ranch in the beautiful Colorado Rockies. Picture a mountain cabin that looked like it came right out of a home decorator magazine. Five-star accommodations meant all our meals were prepared by the camp's private chef. We also had room service, day and night. We were pampered all week and in the lap of luxury. But at that week's end, we packed up and had to head right to the next "camp."

San Diego didn't sound bad to anyone. But that was just the staging area—no trips to the beach. We were only there for about an hour after we landed. At the airport, we joined a number of other families flying in. When the last families arrived, we all got on old school buses. Then we were driven across the border into Tijuana, Mexico.

For a week, we'd been spoiled at a five-star camp. Now we pulled into a large dirt lot where we were given a tent to set up. We went from "power showers" and hot towels to taking "showers" from buckets of water and pretty rough portable toilets. Our food was handed to us in baggies, not served on china. And each day of camp, from (literally) dawn until dark, we joined with five other families to make a team. Each team was tasked with building a house in the barrios from the ground up. To add to the difficulty of not having any power tools or electricity, almost none of us had any real construction experience, except the one master builder assigned to each home.

The family whose home we were building actually lived on the back of the lot where their house would go. Four children and their parents were living in a cardboard shack with a tin roof. Our job was to build them a real house and hand them the keys to their new home at the end of the week. Their first home ever.

For that to happen, however, every man, woman, and child, every minute of every day (with breaks for the kids), worked to dig and pour a foundation. Put up the walls and roof. Then on the last day, while many were inside floating the sheet rock and putting in windows, doors, and cabinets, an eleven-year-old and I were trying to stucco the outside of the house. And we were failing.

There was no cement mixer or power tools (nor the gas or electricity to run them if they'd been there). So we'd dug and sawed and hammered and mixed everything by hand all week. It was too dangerous to stay in the barrios at night, so the leaders had a zero-tolerance policy forcing us to leave at dark when the buses departed whether we were finished with the day's work or not.

It was the last day. We were losing daylight. My arms were shaking from spreading the concrete stucco. We weren't going to make it. My head dropped. Then I looked up and saw an angel standing shoulder to shoulder with me. Actually, it was another man who seemed to have come out of nowhere. Then another man ran up. Then another. Each of them with a trowel. They were from teams who had finished their houses, had been told we needed help, and came running to ours.

Picture now a throng of men, women, and children showing up, helping mix concrete and get the stucco up to finish the outside. Many others inside were getting everything done. Finally, the master builder was finishing the front door frame and getting help hanging the front door.

Then it was over. All except for handing over the key. As we were the last house finished, that involved the whole "team of teams" crowding around. Crying. Hugging each other and that precious family. Handing them the keys to their new home and getting on our buses. Just as the sky turned dark.

We were taken back across the border to a hotel that night. Real beds. Real sheets and pillows. Real bathrooms. In the morning, we had a few hours to kill before our flight left for home. Cindy and I and our girls filled our plates from the amazing buffet at the hotel. We all sat at a table outside, overlooking the ocean in San Diego. And the four of us talked about the last two weeks.

Kari was in junior high. To be honest, she had cried and begged *not* to leave the five-star camp. The camp director had asked her to stay for another week and help out with the horses, which would have been a dream for her. But she'd come as well as her sister. Neither of them had ever slept on the ground before. Or "showered" from a bucket. Or worked all day, every day, for a week. With zero five-star comforts. But then again, they had never played with kids who lived in a cardboard shack. Or seen the tears when a family was handed the keys to a new home.

I wasn't sure what we'd hear from them when I asked them which camp they liked best. I shouldn't have been surprised. It wasn't even close.

They loved their time at the five-star camp, riding horses, being pampered, meeting new friends. But the second camp—and the way they looked at their home and particularly their own rooms when they got home and ever since—changed their lives and ours in many ways.

That group, Amour Ministries, is still doing "family camps" and building homes for the poor today. What they did for our family regarding all of us learning about future-focused serving was priceless. Opening our eyes to serve those in another country. Helping encourage them toward a special future.

You don't have to build a home with your children to help them get the idea they can affect another country. Or be forever grateful for life in their own. But look for ways that you can step into service for your country, such as heading down to help hurricane or tornado victims. Helping build a school on a reservation or handing out turkey dinners for the Salvation Army or local food bank on Thanksgiving. Don't be surprised if your child also does something—even something as small as writing a letter—that can impact the world.

Future-Focused Service *for Our World*

In Malala Yousafzai's country of Pakistan, young women were not permitted to go to school. Defying this ban on learning, Malala went to an "underground" school where she was being taught to read and write. Radicals found out about it and about her. On her way to school one day, she was shot in the head by the Taliban and left for dead. Thankfully, she didn't die. But her terrible plight caught the world's attention. Today, Malala is working towards her bachelor's degree at Oxford. Her charity work through her foundation, The Malala Fund, is helping young women in her country, and in countries all over the world, gain an education.

Thankfully, in most countries in the world, the challenges facing a young person aren't life-and-death ones. But don't underestimate how a child, even your child, can do something that can impact their country and beyond!

Take Samantha Smith, for example. She was only ten years old when the Cold War between the United States and Russia was at its peak. Tensions were so great, many boomers today still remember the air-raid drills run at every US school. The whole class would get under their desks, simulating what they'd do in case of a nuclear attack on their city.

Samantha loved to write. And she felt led to do something with her words. With the world on edge, she wrote a letter to Yuri Andropov, the general secretary of the Soviet Union. In the letter she suggested that both countries could coexist peacefully. Her letter ended up getting published in a Soviet newspaper. Andropov responded with an invitation for Smith and her family to visit his country, *which they did!* This experience earned her the role of "America's youngest ambassador." After her untimely death in a plane crash at only thirteen, monuments in both her Maine hometown and Russia were built in her honor.

Perhaps our child's words won't help to push back a nuclear war—but Samantha's words didn't hurt! You can encourage your children to use their words, or hands, or creativity to go help change their world, to believe our world can have a special future ahead of it as well. That doesn't mean putting pressure on your child to do something a million people will see. Changing the world for the better might simply mean loving one child well.

So ends your first day of class on this fifth element of being relationally intelligent, seeking to build a future-focused willingness to serve others. This takes us now to a starting point, not an ending point. For in the next chapter, we'll help you start building your own plan for learning and living out these five elements with your children!

Chapter 8

Your Starting Point Plan for Applying Relational Intelligence

If you've decided to read this chapter at the end of each element, welcome to how to build out your starting point plan for *application*! Or if you've decided to go through all five elements before beginning, let's give you an outline of what's in this starting point plan.

Your plan links with each of the five elements of relational intelligence for children that you've begun to "go to school" on. You will start by making a plan for ongoing application for *attachment*, which is foundational for anyone wanting to build or live out strong relationships. That gives your children a platform for *exploration*, which is key to their learning new information and your really seeing their strengths. But any time our children take the risk to explore (or we take the risk as parents to allow it), there's a good chance they will stumble or fall down with their early efforts, which is why they need *resilience*. As those three wise life skills are strengthened, they can each provide tremendous help in wise *decision-making* and even building self-regulation. And finally, as a child grows in the ability to do relationships well, the end goal isn't narcissism or total self-interest, but *service* for others, based on a positive future-focused desire to change our relationships and our world for the better.

That's a capsule summary of the whole book. But don't be

overwhelmed by thinking you have to hold every element out in front of your child, each day, for your child to become relationally intelligent. These five elements seen in relationally intelligent homes are not a fool-proof formula. Nor is building out your plan the start of a sprint. As we've said in each main chapter, we're launching a lifelong journey of learning with these elements. So what's the best way to approach this plan?

Just let life come to you!

There may be a week with one child when something comes up at school that becomes a perfect teaching point for attachment. Because it's in your mind as something important and you've made a basic plan, it can be a teaching moment that you capture, not miss! Then something will come up the next week with your other child that provides a great life and learning moment for decision-making. With a plan, you can also find life tossing you a chance to be even better at being resilient or looking for ways to serve others.

It's important to remember: "Principles without practice are pointless." The lack of action certainly doesn't teach relational intelligence! This isn't about "capacity learning"—even if you're super smart and capable of holding loads of information in your mind. Our world is awash with more information than we could ever hope to put our arms around. But it's time now, as we've shared in every chapter at length, to *apply* these skills at wise living! Our plans will be imperfect (because we're all imperfect) and will need to be updated and changed (because we will learn much in its implementation and study)—but making a plan at all is still light-years better than just trying to hold every thought about every element in your mind.

How Your Starting Point Plan Can Be Crafted

Teaching your child to be relationally intelligent is about coaching and encouraging these five elements to be lived out. Your plan can be a great help in doing just that.

You can choose to complete your plan online at www.therelation allyintelligentchild.com where you can capture your evaluations, insights, and thoughts. Or you can build it right here in the book if you do better with a journal experience. And speaking of journals, if you want to use one with *real* paper and pencil or pen, our very favorite journals are found close to the first Starbucks store ever in the Pike Street Market in Seattle. Although we encourage a visit to that iconic Starbucks and the super-fun Fish Market, if you don't live in Seattle, you can check them out online. (And no, we don't get a kickback for recommending these journals. We just think they're outstanding tools that are easy to carry around. Go to www.noboundariesbooks.com.)

Choose a smaller-size journal if you don't want to have to carry this book around. We've taken the plan below and put it in a PDF that you can print off and glue or tape into your favorite size journal. You can find it by going to www.therelationallyintelligentchild.com.

With each element, here's an overview of four things we'll be asking you to do:

1. To evaluate how that element is being lived out right now.
2. To come up with one applicational idea to put into practice.
3. To anticipate one thing that could block your child from applying that element.
4. And a very special feature of this book is the opportunity for you to take a short-form version of the Connect Assessment, a tool we've especially created to help you understand your and your child's unique, God-given strengths. Each child you'll be working with to strengthen their relational intelligence is a unique gift from God. Your children may look alike, but they're likely very different personalities. Let's dig deeper into why becoming a student of your child's strengths can be a tremendous help as you build out their plan.

Why Understanding Personalities Is Important to Learning and Teaching Relational Intelligence

We purposefully wrote this book to help you and your children learn five basic, fundamental elements for becoming more relationally intelligent. Although this book focuses on relational intelligence, we also strongly believed we couldn't fully accomplish our goals without taking a brief look at how personalities tend to affect our learning and applying the five elements.

Doing life together with other people would be incredibly boring if we all had the same personality. Then again, doing life with people different from us can also be challenging and stressful. For example, people who plow their way through tasks, making decisions before consulting others, tend to cause a lot of stress to people who prefer moving slowly and making joint decisions in order to escape any possible pitfalls. The same can be said about those moving slowly by those who prefer moving fast!

So since it's impossible to avoid interacting with people different from us, wouldn't life be much more enjoyable if we better understood and appreciated each other's differences instead of judging character because their actions are so different from ours?

As parents, you already know what it's like trying to successfully blend the different personality types within your household. Although you may have already figured it out, our history of helping families tells us many people are still trying to learn as they go. If that describes you, we believe what you're about to learn can greatly help you and your children clearly understand and apply the five elements of relational intelligence we have just discussed in the previous chapters.

Years ago, Dr. Trent created and introduced to the world a very sensible and fun approach in understanding how personalities affect relationships, using four animals: the Lion, Otter, Golden Retriever, and Beaver. Since then, many thousands of people across the globe have benefited from Dr. Trent's work. In 2015, Dr. Wilson began giving the assessment a new look, and with Dr. Trent's blessing, soon created the Connect Assessment®, which you and your children will soon take and receive your own individual graph.

So, in order to help you better understand what those graphs mean, we will give you a quick overview of four possible graphs next. However, should you like to learn more information about each animal or receive a complete report of your and your children's Connect Assessment®, we recommend you visit therelationallyintelligentchild.com.

Before giving you insights about the following four graphs, it is important for you to know that each of us are a blend of all four animals. Even so, while each of us are a blend, we are also created with certain dominant personality characteristics that tend to impact our behavior the most. So, considering you're about to begin putting your plan together for implementing the five specific elements of relational intelligence, we thought it best to share how each of the following dominant personality types tend to behave in these five elements, beginning with the Lion.

Lion Tendencies

Lions prefer moving at a faster pace and getting things done more quickly than the other three personality types. They tend to view many tasks as challenges and will seldom back away when things get difficult. Because of this and the fact they generally get back up when knocked down, they are considered fairly resilient. Lions are able to make quick decisions when needed, but that doesn't necessarily mean that every decision they make is wise. They tend to make decisions based on how best to complete the job in front of them for the sake of completing the job more than for the people associated with the job or task.

Lions are naturally independent risk-takers and seldom have a problem with launching out to explore their environments. Lions typically do not struggle to interact with others socially. They enjoy talking about their achievements and like being around others who act impressed or compliment them for their accomplishments. Because

Lions are good at getting things done, service to others can look more like making things happen than helping those being served.

Lions can be helped best by slowing down and learning to experience life's events more fully. Not every decision has to be made immediately. Lions tend to respond better if you build them up before pointing out their mistakes or wrongdoings. Give Lions time to process what they hear and then ask them what they heard. Should that be unsuccessful at first, ask them to look at you when you speak to them.

Try hard to not give them too much information at once, and ensure you are speaking in a lower tone. As you can see, Lions naturally possess some of what's needed to be relationally intelligent. However, these perceived characteristics can be overshadowed by their independent, often selfish, motives and behavior. Helping them use their gifts for the sake of others will likely produce quick results for the Lion.

Otter Tendencies

Like Lions, Otters are also fast-paced. However, instead of being independent, they love interacting with people because they naturally attach to others. They tend to deeply internalize their emotions when others refuse to attach to them, primarily seeing these responses as rejection. When this occurs, Otters either withdraw or become verbally critical of those they believe are rejecting them. Because they are so people-oriented, Otters enjoy service to others and will likely make great recruiters because they can be very persuasive. However, like the Lion, they have a tendency to act on selfish motives. Unlike the Lion, they want everyone to like them. They love being on center stage and are often told how wonderful they are.

Because Otters can be emotionally sensitive, some would say that resilience is not a strong asset they possess. However, the Otter will typically stay engaged in the face of adversity. In many instances, the Otter bends rules, which obviously isn't high on the list of making wise decisions. Otters are typically very creative and tend to rapidly explore their environments because they are naturally adventurous.

Otters love to be acknowledged and praised for doing things correctly, so being intentional in this area will motivate them to make wise decisions more often. They do not respond well to authoritative commands, especially when the authority figure uses loud tones or harsh words. Otters generally like discovering new things, so helping them slow down to pay more attention to details can be like giving them many new colors and additional paint brushes to be even more creative. Otters respond well to others who actively participate in the learning process. This generally helps them stay focused and quickly become self-regulating.

Golden Retriever Tendencies

Who doesn't love a Golden Retriever, right? These individuals generally possess a quiet, caring spirit and prefer moving at a slower pace. They typically work hard to do things correctly, simply because it's the right thing to do or for fear of letting others down. They strive for attachment, maybe more than any other personality type. When they feel attached and valued, Golden Retrievers are incredibly loyal—even to their own detriment. On the other extreme, they can feel completely devastated should they believe they are not valued or appreciated. Golden Retrievers are naturally resilient and will stay loyal to the cause or to individuals when many others won't.

When Golden Retrievers are securely attached, they will also work behind the scenes to serve other people. They are generally very sociable but seldom interject their ideas or force themselves on others socially. They prefer being invited to participate. Golden Retrievers are generally good at stepping back to evaluate their circumstances, so they also tend to be wise decision makers. They are predictable, non-confrontational, and do not respond well to risk-taking. Nor do they respond well to being told to simply keep quiet and not ask questions.

Golden Retrievers can be helped best by others demonstrating to them they are valued. They typically respond well to authority figures who treat them with respect, who provide detailed expectations, and who give them ample time to process information in order to make wise decisions. Being forced to follow others who haphazardly make decisions or use loud and abusive language typically causes them to withdraw, shut down, and deeply internalize their emotions. Creating a safe environment, demonstrating love and encouragement for their dedication and hard work will go a long way in helping them self-regulate.

Beaver Tendencies

Beavers also prefer to operate at a slower pace. Like the Lion, while they generally don't demonstrate a high need for attachment, they need the assurance of attachment from caregivers or others close to them. Beavers need time to figure things out—but figure them out they will, typically much better than others because they have the natural ability to analyze details. Beavers tend to not wear their emotions outside for everyone to see. They tend to not complain as quickly as others. They are cautious explorers who generally stick with challenging tasks, exhausting all their resources in order to come to a solution. They enjoy taking things apart just to learn how they work.

At times, Beavers are not seen as risk-takers, but that can be deceiving. Beavers have no problem taking calculated risks. When given time, Beavers will make wise decisions more than not. All the above can go out the window when Beavers do not feel appreciated or valued. They are generally less likely than the other three personality types to initiate a conversation socially. In fact, being forced to interact with people they don't know leaves them feeling very uncomfortable and even anxious. Beavers serve others best by working behind the scenes, mostly fixing things that are broken or putting things together.

Beavers can be helped best through encouragement. They typically put in the effort to do things right, so encouraging words motivate them even more. They respond best to sensible instructions, clearly communicated well in advance. They do not do well being told by authority figures to follow off-the-cuff, spontaneous decisions. When

Beavers feel securely attached, they will explore their world with an engineering mind. Beavers also become bored quickly and are helped when given opportunities to work through challenging projects designed to stretch the imagination.

Instructions for completing your Short Form Connect Assessment can be found at therelationallyintelligentchild.com. Should you like to receive a full report of your and your children's Connect Assessment® report, visit our home page at therelationallyintelligentchild.com for additional instructions.

*** If you have more than one child, please go through this plan focusing on your oldest child first, then go through it for each child in your home.

YOUR STARTING POINT PLAN

The First Element of Relational Intelligence for Children: *Attachment*

When you were ten years old, where would you have put the level of attachment in your home? Circle the number that you feel is most like what you experienced growing up.

1   2   3   4   5   6   7

Very little attachment   Strongly attached

Where are you today when it comes to demonstrating attachment to your child?

1   2   3   4   5   6   7

Do little to purposely   Consistently work to build
build attachment   a strong attachment

Where do you feel your child is at knowing how to build strong attachments with others?

1   2   3   4   5   6   7

Very little or some skill   Relationships come easily

What is one application idea you've seen (in this book or online) that you can apply in your home to strengthen this element?

What is one barrier or struggle you see you're facing in teaching (or in learning yourself) how to live out this element?

Insights Learned from Taking
Your *Short Form Connect Assessment—*
*Relational Intelligence Version**

How do your unique personality strengths impact this element of relational intelligence in your home (making it easier or more difficult for you to live out this element)?

How do your child's unique personality strengths aid or challenge your child in living out this element?

Continuing Education Notes: What insights, examples, suggestions, and application ideas do you want to remember as you look to live this out over time (not overnight)?

The Second Element of Relational
Intelligence for Children: Fearless Exploration

When you were ten years old, where would you have put the level of exploration encouraged in your home? Circle the number that you feel is most like what you experienced growing up.

           1   2   3   4   5   6   7

Very little exploration   Great model shown
                                              for exploration

Where are you today when it comes to demonstrating exploration with your child?

           1   2   3   4   5   6   7

Do little to purposely   Consistently work to
explore them or their world   build exploration

Where do you feel your child is at being open to exploration?

           1   2   3   4   5   6   7

Very little or some skill   Exploration comes easily

What is one application idea you've seen (in this book or online) that you can apply in your home to strengthen this element?

What is one barrier or struggle you see you're facing in teaching (or in learning yourself) how to live out this element?

Insights Learned from Taking
Your *Short Form Connect Assessment—*
*Relational Intelligence Version**

How do your unique personality strengths impact this element of relational intelligence in your home (making it easier or more difficult for you to live out this element)?

How do your child's unique personality strengths aid or challenge your child in living out this element?

Continuing Education Notes: What insights, examples, suggestions, and application ideas do you want to remember as you look to live this out over time (not overnight)?

The Third Element of
Relational Intelligence for Children:
Unwavering Resilience

When you were ten years old, would you say you were encouraged to be resilient in positive ways? Circle the number that you feel is most like what you experienced growing up.

1   2   3   4   5   6   7

Very little encouragement   Good model/teaching
                                              to be resilient

Where are you today when it comes to demonstrating resilience to your child?

1   2   3   4   5   6   7

Do little to purposely   Consistently work to build/
show/build resilience   show resilience

When facing challenges, how resilient is your child?

1   2   3   4   5   6   7

Little or no resilience   Very resilient

What is one application idea you've seen (in this book or online) that you can apply in your home to strengthen this element?

What is one barrier or struggle you see you're facing in teaching (or in learning yourself) how to live out this element?

Insights Learned from Taking
Your *Short Form Connect Assessment—*
*Relational Intelligence Version**

How do your unique personality strengths impact this element of relational intelligence in your home (making it easier or more difficult for you to live out this element)?

How do your child's unique personality strengths aid or challenge your child in living out this element?

Continuing Education Notes: What insights, examples, suggestions, and application ideas do you want to remember as you look to live this out over time (not overnight)?

The Fourth Element of
Relational Intelligence for Children:
Wise Decision-Making

When you were ten years old, where would you have put the level of coaching or encouragement you had in learning wise decision-making in your home? Circle the number that you feel is most like what you experienced growing up.

1   2   3   4   5   6   7

Very little coaching   Often was taught
                                                          or coached

Where are you today when it comes to demonstrating wise decision-making with your child?

1   2   3   4   5   6   7

Do little to purposely   Consistently work to
teach/coach   build strong decision-making

Where do you feel your child is at knowing how to make wise decisions?

1   2   3   4   5   6   7

Very little or some skill   Consistently makes wise choices

What is one application idea you've seen (in this book or online) that you can apply in your home to strengthen this element?

What is one barrier or struggle you see you're facing in teaching (or in learning yourself) how to live out this element?

Insights Learned from Taking
Your *Short Form Connect Assessment—*
*Relational Intelligence Version**

How do your unique personality strengths impact this element of relational intelligence in your home (making it easier or more difficult for you to live out this element)?

How do your child's unique personality strengths aid or challenge your child in living out this element?

Continuing Education Notes: What insights, examples, suggestions, and application ideas do you want to remember as you look to live this out over time (not overnight)?

The Fifth Element of
Relational Intelligence for Children:
Future-Focused Service

When you were ten years old, where would you have put the level of service to others in your home? Circle the number that you feel is most like what you experienced growing up.

1   2   3   4   5   6   7

Very little modeled   Service to others was obvious/
                                                     often modeled

Where are you today when it comes to demonstrating service to your child?

1   2   3   4   5   6   7

Do little to purposely   Consistently work to
serve others   model serving others

Where do you feel your child is at knowing how to serve others?

1   2   3   4   5   6   7

Very little or some skill   Service comes easily

What is one application idea you've seen (in this book or online) that you can apply in your home to strengthen this element?

What is one barrier or struggle you see you're facing in teaching (or in learning yourself) how to live out this element?

Insights Learned from Taking
Your *Short Form Connect Assessment—*
*Relational Intelligence Version**

How do your unique personality strengths impact this element of relational intelligence in your home (making it easier or more difficult for you to live out this element)?

How do your child's unique personality strengths aid or challenge your child in living out this element?

Continuing Education Notes: What insights, examples, suggestions, and application ideas do you want to remember as you look to live this out over time (not overnight)?

Great Parents Are Like Great Coaches

If you have ever played any type of organized sports, whether individual or team, we bet a dollar to a doughnut you can name one or more of your favorite coaches along with telling us what you believe made them great. Or maybe you've seen movies like *Remember the Titans, We Are Marshall,* or *Coach Carter.* If you haven't seen these or any movies like them, we highly recommend you do! Mainly because some of the common principles that made all these coaches really good can also help make you a really good parent! And if you remember from previous chapters, the more you rehearse what you learn in your mind, the more likely they are to become automatic thoughts and beliefs that will drive your behavior.

Really Good Parents Focus on Their Children First

Being so focused on self is a really big reason why so many parents today struggle to have good parent-child relationships. It's next to impossible to give attention to your children's needs or monitor their activities that lead to unhealthy behaviors when the majority of your attention is dedicated to meeting your needs and desires based on self-entitlement. Sounds a little harsh, we know. But your children are your responsibility and assignment from God, who gave them to you and entrusted you with their well-being. Most parents have eighteen years or less to prepare their children for the rest of their lives. Begin today by making a commitment to learn, teach, and model relationally intelligent skills to your child even when your perceived self-entitlements seem more important.

Really Good Parents Parent Proactively—Not Reactively

The moment of crisis is not the time to find out whether your child has what it takes to successfully navigate through challenges. This is why too many parents today have become "snowplow" parents. There will be times when you will need to make training your child in the elements of relational intelligence more demanding and challenging so they'll be better prepared to cope with the crises ahead of them.

Really Good Parents Develop and Learn

Good parents realize how dynamic the world in which our children are growing up truly is. The pressures associated with the ever-changing environments impacting our children can easily become greater than our abilities to parent them through these changes. Therefore, you will need to commit to be a long-term learner who consistently evaluates your parenting abilities. Considering how easy it is for your children to access information online, as well as how quickly the information they are exposed to is changing, staying ahead of them will require intentionality on your part. Remember: "Perceived need drives intentionality." Knowing what your children are potentially exposed to before they become exposed will determine your intentionality.

Really Good Parents Make Mid-Course Corrections

As your children learn to become more relationally intelligent, your teaching and training plan will likely need to be modified in order to maximize their future performance. Coaches hold weekly staff meetings to purposefully evaluate recent performances and then determine the correct mid-course correction needed to better succeed moving forward. You will need to consistently evaluate your child's performance and be willing to modify and adapt new strategies as your child develops.

No one said this type of parenting is easy. But just as the best coaches know themselves and their players really well, the same can be said for you and your children. By recognizing your and each child's characteristic strengths, consistently monitoring your attitudes, and being willing to make the five characteristics your automatic thoughts, we believe you will have the effective foundational tools needed for helping your child become more relationally intelligent. The effort you put forth will no doubt make you more relationally intelligent and give you greater self-confidence not only as a parent, but also in every other role you have in life.

Tools to Help You Succeed in the Days to Come

Great work on beginning to build out your plan! But we wouldn't be very good guides if we took you from the airport to the center of town and then just dropped you off and said, "Good luck with that!"

We want to help you keep being successful in learning and living out your relational intelligence with your children. The last section of the book can help you do just that. Three barriers can block you from building out, living out, or even starting to apply your plan. After learning how to avoid those, you'll be encouraged by three gifts that can be extremely helpful in your continued success.

Finally, the last chapter leads us to where the fifth element of relational intelligence should always lead us. Not just in building up our own skills at relating well with others for our sake, or even just for the benefit of our children. Our final call to action for you is to reach out. Pick another family in your life, someone in your neighborhood or on the base where you're living, a small group or life-group friend, or even one of your beloved siblings whom you know in your heart of hearts would benefit from what you're learning and living—for we always learn best that which we have to teach.

Chapter 9

Three Currents That Can Stop You from Becoming Relationally Intelligent

You've read through the importance of having relational skills for yourself and your children. Along with the five core elements, you now have a picture in your mind of how children and their parents reflect relational intelligence. In addition, you've started building a plan for application, including how each person's personality tends to impact one or all of the five core elements of relational intelligence.

But if you're going to be truly successful in coaching and modeling these five elements, it's important to be prepared to face three predictable challenges that can keep you and your child from living out relational intelligence. We're not saying these three are the only challenges, but they are predictable challenges that many parents and families face. And forewarned is forearmed. Also know that each challenge can be overcome, beginning with the first challenge, which is all about the cultures we swim in . . .

Unseen Currents Can Direct Our
Lives Away from Relational Intelligence

Learning how to scuba dive was on my (Dewey's) bucket list for more than forty years. I suppose it's because growing up in the 1960s, I loved watching a show called *Sea Hunt*. In almost every episode, super-frog-man Mike Nelson was miraculously rescuing someone trapped deep underwater or saving the world from nuclear attack. Amazingly, he would accomplish it in thirty minutes every week (minus the breakfast cereal commercials). Basically, he was the 1960s version of Aquaman, only without the amazing special effects.

I finally reached my personal goal of becoming a frogman when I was open-water certified at the age of sixty. I continued on to get my advanced open-water certification and today, diving with my oldest daughter and her husband has rapidly become my favorite hobby. It is simply breathtaking to navigate weightlessly fifty to one hundred feet underwater, watching countless species of fish feeding on coral that is alive with almost every color known to man. It's wonderful to feel *free* to explore our underwater world!

But then I tried something called "drift diving."

Drift diving has become increasingly more popular in recent years. It involves divers jumping into the ocean from a boat before descending thirty to eighty feet where there are known currents. Before they know it, divers find themselves getting carried along in a current deep underwater in the midst of a huge ocean. Then, after thirty to forty-five minutes of being propelled along, sometimes at pretty good speeds, these divers swim out of the current and start making their way to the surface where the same boat they bailed out of earlier is waiting for them. Or that's the way drift diving should go . . . theoretically.

The first time I heard about drift diving, I remember thinking, *I could get used to that!* Being effortlessly carried along by a current as I take in all the amazing sights. That sounded like a great ride at Disneyland or Universal Studios, only underwater. So I jumped at the first opportunity to go drift diving in the Caribbean Ocean. Unfortunately, the reality of my first experience drift diving didn't pan out the way it should have theoretically. Instead, I experienced a lot of strong currents that forced me to go places I didn't want to go.

On the boat, our dive master failed to mention the strength of the currents we were about to catch. We geared up, jumped into the water, and started going down. I could see the coral approximately forty feet below. I didn't immediately recognize any significant currents and figured it was going to be a nice, peaceful dive. But as we got closer to the bottom, things began to change quickly when we all swam into a pretty strong current.

Within minutes, I began seeing some pretty cool things and wanted to stop and check them out. But before I knew it, the current had pushed me too far away and the opportunity to explore what I wanted was gone. At times, I attempted to swim back against the current, hoping to check out what I previously saw, only to give up because I was burning through the air in my tank that I would need to safely get back to the surface. I'm in pretty good shape for my age, but because the current was so strong, even the younger divers were beginning to run low on air, so we had to make our way to the surface.

Throughout the whole experience, it was unnerving to realize that something *invisible* could become such a determining factor in where I was going, taking control of my direction and my choices. Leading me places I didn't necessarily want to go and past things I really wanted to see. It was like walking with a stiff wind at your back that's not so noticeable until the moment you want to change direction and realize the wind is doing everything it can to forcefully push you back in that one direction.

This may sound a little dramatic, but we want you to know that we understand how challenging it is to fight through different types of currents when you're physically and emotionally exhausted and all you want to do is get to a place where you can finally quit fighting and find *rest*. We'll come back to that word in a moment.

I'm absolutely going to keep scuba diving, but I'm pretty much "one and done" with drift diving if future dives are at all like my last experience. One good thing about this challenge was it made me a better diver. That's what most challenges do. They make us better when we allow them to. It also gave me a pretty good picture of what each of us as parents, spouses, and friends can experience in life.

Getting Caught in a Current

What do we mean by "culture"? Sometimes movies become icons for what's going on in a culture. Take the movie *Mean Girls* or similar movies, like *Legally Blonde* or *The Devil Wears Prada*.

Who hasn't walked into a new school, or new workplace, or showed up for a first practice with a new sports team? By lunchtime on our first day at work or by the end of the first practice, we're starting to understand that every job, every team, has both a written and an unwritten job description.

For example, bullying wasn't written down in the student handbook at North Shore High School, the fictitious setting for *Mean Girls*. But for any of us who have survived junior high or high school, from our first day on campus, we began to understand there *is* a culture in that school. Something very real. Yet again, very much unwritten.

"Culture" then is like a current moving through school. You didn't see it stenciled on the walls outside, but once you're inside, it's a strong-arm way of demanding, "This is the way relationships are done here." Today's culture can seem like an irresistible force capable of doing real damage to our choices, our relationships, and our children's future.

Let's look at the first thing that can keep us from pursuing health and life and relational intelligence for our child. And that's the culture we grew up in—or the one our children are swimming in right now.

The Culture We Swim in Can Push Us Away from Healthy Relationships

We are immersed in the culture we live in today. However, it's not easy to "see" the impact it can make on us becoming relationally intelligent.

In fact, it's much easier to just drift along with whatever current culture is saying about how we should do relationships. Easier than stopping and considering what's real and right.

If we never question what culture tells us is "right" or healthy, it can cause us to rush right past what really brings health and healing, hope and relational life. Even *rest* for our souls!

The prophet Jeremiah, commenting on the culture around him in his day, highlighted what many people were feeling. "Superficially, [they say], 'Peace, peace,' But there is no peace" (see Jer. 8:11).

Doesn't that sound like life today? It offers so much—yet countless kids and parents are following along in the cultural currents that are pushing them toward loneliness, depression, discouragement, and defeat!

Yet as we've seen, there is so much *real* help today. So many clinical studies on what actually makes close, caring relationships. So many powerful links to timeless biblical truths that support or illustrate those current studies!

Jeremiah goes on to say, "This is what the LORD says: 'Stand by the ways and see and ask for the ancient paths, where the good way is, and walk in it; *then you will find a resting place for your souls*'" (Jer. 6:16, our emphasis).

There's that word again. Rest. There's a huge benefit of following timeless truths on what can help us strengthen attachment and love. That encourages us to let our child safely but realistically explore. That builds resilience and results in wise decision-making and serving others: the building blocks of strong relationships.

While speaking of his spiritual family, the apostle John says something that is true of every parent: "I have no greater joy than this, to hear of my children walking in the truth" (3 John 1:4). Imagine walking out from a basketball game your child just played in, and another parent comes up and says, "Hey, I just want you to know something. Your kid is an amazing person. She was over to our house with our daughter, helping her with her homework the other day. She is so bright, caring, and humble, and just a joy to be around."

You hear something like that, and emotionally it takes you, even if just for a moment, to a place of rest. Your kids aren't perfect. But as they learn how to do relationships well, to really love and build attachment, care, resilience, courage, and optimism, the way God intends for them as they model how to love and live like Jesus, every step they take toward relational intelligence can bring "rest" to their soul and yours.

It's been said that parents are about as happy as their saddest kid. So many kids today are drifting along, feeling like relational orphans.

> *To live out what you've learned about relational intelligence, it's important to look at the culture we're living in, and radically accept what you find and learn there.*

So we want to urge you to fight back against any culture (past or present) that defines relationships in a way that leads to brokenness, not walking in truth and life.

A powerful insight on getting a clear purpose and direction for life is found in Dr. Deborah Gorton's book, *Embracing Uncomfortable*.[1] She calls men and women to live out "radical acceptance." That is to nail down a "true north" in your life, as we've laid down these five clear measures of relational intelligence. But then she talks about how important it is to face up to issues that make us uncomfortable. And when we do, as Dr. Gorton teaches her counseling students and clients, we can begin to "get comfortable with being uncomfortable."

Take dieting as a pretty universal example. When does the average person quit a diet? It's when it becomes "uncomfortable."

As we consider this idea of looking honestly at the culture we live in, we may decide that health and living out relational intelligence are countercultural to much of what's being said! We may need to get "comfortable" with the idea that it's going to be "uncomfortable" trying to swim out of the cultural currents and toward health and life.

Let's take a look at several of the most recent generations to help this become more real and visible in how we do relationships.

A Look at Several Cultural Currents

We can't do much more than provide a basic look at this idea of culture vs. health and life. But again, if you want more, head to our website at www.therelationallyintelligentchild.com or look at the appendix where we'll list several very helpful books to go much deeper.

We'll start with the silent generation on through Gen Z. Part of being "relationally intelligent" is being able to move toward people who are different from us. It can be really helpful to look at what has affected people all up and down the age spectrum.

THE SILENT GENERATION (1929–1945)

- Experienced the Great Depression and the great challenges of World War II

- Humble and grateful to have food and work

- Respected and trusted authority

- Strong family and community relationships

- The "silent" comes from a cultural current of not sharing feelings or hurts, just putting your head down and "doing the hard work" before you

- Technology advances: automobiles, radio, movies, airplanes

This was the generation that saw the explosion of transportation technology change their world. In their lifetime, automobiles took over for wagons. For example, many people of this generation experienced traveling in a wagon from one location to another as a child, but would later fly over those same roads in a commercial airliner. That's a lot of change in one lifetime! Life was much more communal during that day, with people depending on others to harvest and build schools and infrastructure. Knowledge was often limited by where people lived and who was around them. What people did in life was most often linked to what their parents did. Relationally, divorce was almost unheard of and families spent far more time together than today.

But spending time together didn't necessarily mean bonding or closeness. There was also a strong message in this generation to "Don't talk about it—just do it." Just "Put your head down and keep going" enabled people to struggle through the terrible losses of the Great Depression and the incredible challenges in fighting and winning World War II. Loyalty and commitment were very strong, as they are indeed part of building strong relationships today. But emotions were often stuffed down. So too were praise and encouragement in many cases. You might "see it" but you didn't "say it." Performance and conformity were often valued more than care and unconditional acceptance. "You can count on me to put food on the table but not to talk at the table."

BABY BOOMERS (1946–1964)

- Post WWII and Great Depression—time of prosperity

- 79 million babies born

- Civil Rights movement and rebellion against authority

- Strong push for consumerism

- Employment and educational status were means to status and success

- Family values were challenged due to drugs (Woodstock), the "sexual revolution," and protest of the Vietnam War

- Technology meant supremacy: television, satellites, computers, space travel, nuclear bombs

These may be your parents or grandparents. They grew up in a current that was in many ways reacting to the *scarcity mentality* of the silent generation. Millions came back from the war having seen the world, ready to push back boundaries on learning and convention. For example, women had stepped into the workplace and factories and many would not go back home in the way or numbers they had in the past. Plants that once ran nonstop, building tanks and cranking out war matériel, now turned that massive capacity toward building consumer cars, trucks, and appliances. Meeting the huge demand for new things fit right in with a major push toward consumerism. People began to openly question "the ways things were." This is the generation when the civil rights movement began, when the protests against our overseas involvement in the Vietnam War rocked the nation. Women's rights rallies and more sprang up. And a common cry heard during this time was "Never trust anyone over thirty."

Relationally, this was a time when communal living was overtaken by the push for individual rights. When people began to say "no" to the status quo. That led to the hard fought but important movement toward freedom and rights for all. But all that struggle, all that anger, all that push toward "freedom" simultaneously led to a "free love" culture that devalued marriage and commitment. "Love the one you're with" didn't look at what was left when someone moved on to the next person. People were demanding a voice. But brokenness began to grow as families and the inner city began to come apart. Although boomers have stockpiled more wealth than any generation in our history, so much of their focus was on getting "things" which resulted in relationships often taking a backseat to work. Family attachment was sacrificed for individual gain.

GEN X (1965–1979)

- Individual rights moved center stage—with LGBT, women's, and workplace rights being voiced.

- Family values became greatly diminished. No-fault divorce explodes and the "Great Society" tries to help the poor, yet actually incentivizes couples not to marry. Divorce

becomes a new normal, and abortion is legalized, along
with more questioning of authority.

- As a reaction to the boomers' focus on workaholism and
  the accumulation of "things," Gen Xers begin to look at
  work as a necessity but not an endgame. Watching the
  boomers build so much, yet at such a cost to relationships,
  causes many to decide workaholism is not a great choice.

- Social identity becomes even more shaped by MTV, music,
  and early online platforms.

- Known as digital immigrants, they grow up without computer technology, but rush to use mobile telephones and
  personal computers as they come out.

Gen X individuals grew up in a culture where the strong push for
individual rights and a questioning of absolutes was the norm. Here
the first drumbeat of "moral relativism" really echoed in the culture.
What's "right" for *you* took precedence—right and wrong became
outdated absolutes and only concepts derived from religion or culture.
Individual rights continued their ascendancy. The word *codependency*
became a cultural buzzword that questioned even healthy attachment. Without realizing the damage coming later with loneliness and
depression, "I'll do it my way" was pushed as being more important
than doing it together. With marriages crumbling even more, and the
results of the sexual revolution leaving many "let's not talk about it"
victims, brokenness became rampant. Dramatic events like Watergate
began destroying trust in politicians to heal all our hurts, and the
church came under attack in ways it never had before. Hollywood
rushed to question limits and push any boundaries reminiscent of the
past out of the way.

MILLENNIALS (1980–1989—older millennials)
                       (1990–1996—younger millennials)

- Worldview is now fully engaged in "I'm most important."

- Many are told by parents, eager to push aside any limits, that for their child "anything is possible"—but don't link that to the work ethic of boomers or commitment of the silent generation to reach their goals.

- Instead, participation trophies and hovering parents try to erase the barriers that, if climbed by their children, could help create resiliency.

- Employment goals now become more about serving and making a difference—someone else will figure out how to raise the finances needed to make it happen.

- Distrust in authority led them to become very selective in who/what to follow.

- They experienced the 2008 recession where many saw their parents suffer and even lose their homes. Hence they developed no strong confidence that society or politicians could offer any real security for the average person. This lack of security became national as well as personal with the continued breakdown of the family.

- Older millennials were the last digital immigrants, meaning they were born not having computers, the internet, and cellphones.

- Younger millennials are the first digital natives—people who have never not had computers, the internet, social media, and cellphones.

- Relationships, in just a decade, have begun to dramatically transition from face-to-face (interpersonal) to online "relationships" on Facebook, Google, and LinkedIn.

- They have become even stronger advocates for people having a "choice" in their lifestyles and going their own way, even if that way leads to brokenness or damaged relationships.

This group is so large, it needs to be divided into two parts. Older millennials still have one foot in the world of tradition and absolutes from past generations, and for them technology is something to adapt to, not just experience, while younger millennials are true digital natives. They, and those after them, have grown up never knowing a time when technology hasn't dominated relationships and the way we do life. They also grew up with "That's OK for you, but there are no real absolutes when it comes to right and wrong." They continue the march toward relational isolation by being great at creating online smiling Facebook images, but not time spent building strong face-to-face relationships.

GENERATION Z (1997–2018)

- These are true digital natives in that smartphones, Facebook, Twitter, Pinterest, Snapchat, etc., are a way of life. This generation of young people are amazing multitaskers—able to talk on the phone while doing homework while texting, while talking to you at the same time.

- Technology is to be mastered, improved, or even reinvented.

- More entrepreneurial than any previous generation, they come up with creative ways—in the workplace and at home—to build wealth through online platforms and connectivity.

- They are much more tolerant of others regarding different ethnicity, sexual orientation, or race. Their only concern about diversity is that it's present.

- After several generations of brokenness, from multiple divorces to the #MeToo explosion to more time spent with people online than face-to-face, to parents making iPads and technology surrogate parents, they have become the most isolated and lonely generation. In some ways, they are the most "unparented" generation ever, as children are put in front of technology and see less and less modeling of face-to-face parenting.

- Relationships are a matter of practicality.

- They are the least likely generation to attend church, but very open to knowing who God is and why He's relevant.

- They believe in thinking for themselves and don't necessarily need/want authority figures.

These digital natives are amazing at multitasking and really want to go out and change their world for the better. Relationally, this generation has an incredible amount of information (almost totally unfiltered) but can lack wisdom or the skill of doing life and relationships well. Moral relativism is pervasive, resulting in their being extremely accepting of different viewpoints, including having a fluid understanding of sexuality and gender identity. Pornography is a normative experience for these people, like wallpaper—it's simply everywhere and available and seen at very early ages. So they have an absence of "childhood" with almost nothing (words/videos/pictures) being withheld from the young. With all the sexual information and misinformation and family brokenness, they have a huge need for attachment and a huge presence of depression and hopelessness. Yet once they see the personal value in attachment and relationships, they can be creative and committed advocates for healthy relations.

With that brief overview of the past ninety-plus years of culture and relationships, you can see why life can be very challenging for parents today! For example, if you're an older millennial parent, raising a Gen Z child, you might think it would be normal and healthy for him or her to look you in the eye when talking to you. But Gen Z children and now young adults have moved miles away from doing relationships that aren't online. They're multitaskers who see nothing wrong with occasionally looking up at you while checking in with their friends and watching a video or doing their homework at the same time.

The way Gen Z looks at faith and life and relationships culturally can be very different than their parents. That doesn't mean you can't step into their lives and help them be relational! But it's important to answer the questions they're asking. For example, Gen Z children are not as focused on "Did Jesus rise from the dead?" The question they're asking now is "So what if He did?"

Your child, of any age, needs strong, connected, secure relationships. Remember, loneliness is the epidemic haunting this generation and possibly your child. It's crucial to understand that their being great at technology isn't the same as their being great at face-to-face relationships. They will need those relational skills in school, the workplace, and their most important relationships.

It's important then to look at where we've grown up. Perhaps even where our parents grew up. But also, it's important to become a student of the current generation and challenges facing the waters our children are swimming in.

By doing so, you can begin to see where you need to push back instead of just floating along toward whatever latest cultural shift is taking place. That doesn't mean you just react to everything culture says to embrace today, but that you learn to be proactive and wise in asking what really *does* lead toward health and life!

Not just accepting everything our culture does to push and direct our lives then is the first challenge we need to face. Let's move on to the next challenge. One that is much more personal, because it's linked directly with your past . . .

Your Past Can Push You Away from Building Close Relationships

Like so many others, I (Dewey) definitely experienced my share of dysfunction in our family. In fact, growing up, my brother and

I (mainly my brother) were constantly into something so mischievous it required our parents to either pay for something or apologize profusely to keep us out of trouble.

Later, during my teenage years, my parents were dealing with so many life issues that I made it my utmost goal to not add to their stress. That means I made the decision to try not to demand a lot of attention—or supervision—from them.

I certainly wasn't challenged to work hard in school, and I easily made Cs with very little studying. The only disadvantage to that was when it came time to go to college. My average grades persuaded my parents that maybe college wasn't for me. I remember my mother commenting in a conversation we were having, "Not everyone is cut out for college."

Now, my mom and dad were wonderful parents. I choose to believe they were doing their best at the time to navigate all the challenges. I eventually did go to college two years after high school, but I withdrew a few years later. Sadly, for almost thirty years, I allowed those words from my past, "Not everyone is cut out for college" to determine my capacity to learn. However, that wouldn't be the end of my academic journey.

I returned to college after a thirty-year intermission in 2010. The guy that could only make Cs in high school graduated with a Bachelor of Science degree magna cum laude, a Master of Arts degree, and was finally awarded a PhD at the age of sixty-one! At the end of the day, I am a living example of what can happen when people are given opportunities to create new abilities—and how words spoken in our past don't have to control our future.

If the culture we swim in can push us away from healthy relationships, so too can events from our own past, including statements or actions that we're still using to define us. Our past can put blinders on us, making it impossible to really see what we're "locked" or pushed into doing relationally—even if it's unhealthy!

James, like nearly half of the young men he went to school with, had his father leave his mother and siblings when he was three years old. Like too many young men, and even more young women, he experienced sexual abuse from an uncle. Carrying all that unprocessed brokenness into college, his senior year he met a young woman with many of the same masking traits. She too had lots of hurt in her background. Her focus was on painting a "Facebook perfect" image for the world, while their lack of relational skills was ruining their relationship.

Three children later, James's marriage had totally fallen apart. That was also when he was diagnosed with and almost died of nonsmoker's lung cancer. The cancer had moved to other places in his body, so he was initially misdiagnosed. But that near-death experience, along with all the hurt from his past and present, caused him to make a decision.

He was sharing custody of the three children. After all the hurt both he and his children had seen and experienced, he decided they'd all seen enough negatives in their lives, so he made an iron-clad "fixed mindset" decision.

When it was their week in his home, they wouldn't hear the word no.

They would find total "acceptance," not discipline.

Sound like a good decision? The softer and softer he became, the more defiant and hard-sided his children became! One of his sons in particular became out-of-control angry and disrespectful.

With all that trauma poured into one life story, you can certainly understand why he would decide that hurt and a strong-side love wasn't something he wanted for his children. But his decision to look at relationships as all softness and no strength put blinders on the way he saw health!

He indeed had enough pain and harshness for two lifetimes. But being unwilling to get comfortable with being uncomfortable or setting some appropriate boundaries on his children's behavior created massive challenges for everyone in his home.

James isn't alone. Many of us let something that has been said or done to us define how we relate to others. The past can affect our belief in what we can learn or become today and cap our future. The unprocessed past can and does shove us into one way of relating.

Take a hard look at your past. Perhaps words spoken in anger by a parent, or even words that were meant to help, have held you back from your potential in life and relationships—as they did for Dewey at the start of this chapter with hearing he just wasn't cut out for learning.

Are we still tied up in knots emotionally from the unhealthy hurts? Is that blocking how we understand what love and close relationships look like when they're lived out in health? Love really does have two sides. A strong side and a soft side both affect our ability to be relationally intelligent.

Take a hard look, then, at the culture you're swimming in. Ask God for the courage to become a student of your past, particularly if you need to "untie the knots" or find freedom to add softness or strength. Here is one more roadblock that impacts far too many people. Three words that can stop us in our tracks in terms of living out relational intelligence.

But You Don't Understand . . . It's Too Late to Do This with My Children

We cannot begin to tell you how many parents we've talked to who in one form or another have shared heartfelt words like the following. "All this about being relational and doing face-to-face relationships is great for our four-year-old. But we're a blended family. We have a thirteen- and fifteen-year-old. They are just unreachable. *If we'd only known or gotten started earlier . . . but it's too late . . .* "

By this point in the book, you've heard us say time and again that you can do this. You can become, yourself, more relationally intelligent and model that for your child. It can be a major challenge to try to step into the life of a child who has been hurt, whether by us, in relationships they had before they got to our home, or by others outside the home. But don't give up. Love covers a multitude of sins. Healing and hope can come. That doesn't mean we can wave a magic wand at past hurts and have them all go away for our child. But seek help. Go to counseling. Join a support group. Pray for them every night. Don't quit providing or enforcing boundaries. Realize that they may not change today, but you are giving them a model of unconditional love and acceptance for tomorrow.

One more thing: Dive into the next chapter as well, where instead of focusing on three challenges, like in this chapter, you'll see three more things that can help and keep you moving forward toward relational intelligence and all the benefits it can bring your child.

Chapter 10

Three Gifts to Succeed in Modeling and Coaching Relational Intelligence

You've learned a great deal about relational intelligence, as well as challenges that can come up against you. But let's close by sharing with you three important gifts that can help you live out each element—starting with the amazing brain you were created with!

What's Neuroplasticity Have to Do with It?

The human brain is the most complex and mysterious organ in the human body. For centuries, scientists and researchers have attempted to understand brain development. In particular, they want to know how it processes data, influences behaviors, and more generally, how the brain interacts with each part of the human body.

The first significant strides in brain research occurred in the late 1800s with the identification of cells in nerve tissue called neurons. Scientists discovered what happens when these neurons connect with each other. Understanding this connection helped scientists understand how we learn, a discovery that resulted in a new scientific field of study called *neuroscience.*

In 1890, the word *plasticity* first appeared in text. It was used to describe how structures in the brain could be influenced to create *new* connections. These new connections were believed to be primarily responsible for the development of new habits and insights. Just as when "attachment" was first presented to those medical and scientific gatekeepers, the idea that you really could learn something new—especially as you grew older—was laughed at by experts of that day.

For example, in 1913, it was asserted that once brain development stopped as a child, neural paths were *fixed* and completely unchangeable over time.[1] In other words, your capacity to learn was "capped" when your brain reached its adult size. Basically, old dogs couldn't learn new tricks.

Amazingly, this view became an unquestionable doctrine held by most neuroscientists until a discovery about neurons in 1998. That's when the startling discovery was made that this idea once floated almost one hundred years earlier—of "neuroplasticity" or the brain's ability to learn new things—was actually true!

This happened when neural stem cells (self-renewing cells) were first discovered in the *adult* brain, showing conclusively that the brain does *not* stop producing neurons or otherwise turn off its learning capacity after five or six years old![2]

This new revelation convincingly reversed almost everything that was previously believed about the brain. Today, along with massive technological advances in brain imagery, neuroplasticity has become front and center in neuroscience research.

What all this means is that neuroplasticity is a God-given, built-in feature in an individual's brain that allows it to continually transform its structure and functionality according to data it receives through repeated experiences. That's at *any* age!

In simple terms, our brain consists of as many as one hundred billion neurons that begin developing months prior to birth and continue throughout our life. These neurons connect with each other to eventually form a dynamic neural circuitry throughout various parts of the brain. These circuits are associated with various functions such as learning, memory, and decision-making, all influencing how we interact with others *relationally*. While most of these neural connections stabilize during childhood, neuroplasticity describes how this dynamic structure is constantly changing all throughout life.

Dr. Philippe Douyon, in his book, *Neuroplasticity: Your Brain's Superpower,* describes what it can mean to us like this:

> Neuroplasticity is . . . the process of how our brains' structure changes in response to *every experience* we have. . . . Neuroplasticity tells us about how we learn, evolve, regress, and recuperate from neurologic injury. . . . It gives us hope that no matter the state of our brains, we can change for the better through a choice of different strategies. Our awareness of the process of neuroplasticity allows us to adapt to our circumstances, creating new and incredible lives for ourselves.[3]

You really can learn and grow. Your children can as well. At any age and stage! And that includes if we've grown up with a lack of relationality, or with abuse, or even under trauma. It's a wonderfully hopeful discovery that we really can change the direction of our thinking and living.

Of course, there's the flip side of neuroplasticity as well. For it's a picture of *how our brains' structure changes in response to every experience we have.* Meaning everything, positive or negative, can build new learning pathways. So, when you and your children are forced to deal with cultural issues like bullying, sexting, violent gaming, and the myriad of relationship dramas occurring on social media, it can also impact their learning and growth toward health.

So as much as possible, it needs to be "out with the bad and in with the good." Understand as well that the learning process doesn't happen overnight. Younger children tend to learn new behaviors and experiences for making new relationships more quickly. For older children, many of their existing neural pathways must first be redirected and new neural pathways established. *This type of training requires time.* Yet, through patience and perseverance, new behaviors can eventually become automatic.

According to Moheb Costandi, a developmental neurobiologist and author of *Neuroplasticity*,

> Training optimizes the brain areas and neural pathways involved in performing a given task; as a result, the individual's performance on that task improves, and the task eventually becomes automatized and effortless.[4]

In other words, all this teaching and learning, when put into practice, really can make a positive difference in how relationships are done in your home! Commitment and consistent effort will lead to positive, hugely beneficial changes.

We've seen that the brain you and your child have is geared to learning new things, which leads to a second positive to keep in mind as well.

The Impact YOU Have on Their Lives

Study after study is showing that nothing—not social media, friends, or even life experiences—has the capacity to affect a child's life in a positive way as much as a parent or primary caregiver. Even so, not all parents buy in to this reality. Many parents consider themselves at the bottom of the list in impacting their children's lives. Yet, when asked, the majority of children listed their parents as having the greatest influence on their life.

One of my (Dewey's) fondest memories is having had the opportunity to coach our oldest daughter's fast pitch softball team from elementary through early high school. It wasn't just about learning to play softball. It was all those conversations about life and relationships, while doing all that traveling to and from different softball fields that is such a powerful memory and blessing to me. But what has shocked me is how much it influenced our daughter as well.

She is in her mid-thirties today with a family of her own. But oftentimes when our favorite teams are playing on TV, we spend a lot of the game texting commentary back and forth. It's as if we were still sitting in the front seat of my truck coming home from softball practice.

Our younger daughter excelled in dance and music, so my wife, Lynne, became her designated agent and driver for more than ten years. Because of the countless number of conversations and shared experiences over those years, today Mom is still the default "go to" person for getting trusted advice on just about everything from fashion to relationships. For both Lynne and me, it wasn't the places we went, but the conversations we had that today keep our relationships so strong.

As we've talked about throughout this book, it's a loving, close-knit relationship that is most linked to childhood happiness.

A Third Key to Succeeding
That Can Change a Loved One's Life as Well

We've looked at how you can keep learning new things about relationships and how you are better positioned than any person on the planet to leave a loving, happy, relational imprint on your child. But now let's lift your eyes to one more thing that can be of tremendous help to *you*—as you become the guide for a family who needs so much to know what you've learned.

We pray for your growth and success in helping each child in your home become stronger at being relationally intelligent. We sincerely hope you'll stay connected with us at therelationallyintelligentchild.com.

Here's our closing challenge that can be such a great way of not just reading about but living out these five elements. That's for you to look around your life, talk it over with your spouse if you're married, and then reach out to help one other family grow in their relationships as well.

It has been often said that we teach best what we most need to learn. You wouldn't have come this far in this book if you weren't serious about learning about relational intelligence. So a great next step would be for you to become the guide and teacher to someone else. Perhaps a neighbor or close friend, a sibling or someone you work with, serve with, or share similar life goals with for your children and their need to be challenged to be more loving, caring, attached, and wise in doing life!

It could be one family or one person. We know people who have started a small group in their home, church, or school. We can't wait to hear about the life or lives you affected in a significant way by helping them become relationally intelligent and how that has helped your family as well!

May the Lord bless and keep you and each child in your home, helping each one in your family live out these five elements in a way that influences and changes your world!

Acknowledgments

W e'd like to acknowledge John Hinkley, acquisitions editor at Moody Publishers, for his guidance, support, and encouragement throughout this project. A special thanks to Kari Stageberg and Laura Morris for their insights in reading and sharing their thoughts on the book. And grateful acknowledgment to Focus on the Family, especially Larry Weeden and Steve Johnson, for their teaming with Moody Publishers, because of their belief in this book and the for relational intelligence need in children and their parents' lives today.

NOTES

Chapter 1: The Incredible Gift You Can Give a Child

1. Marisa Donnelly, "36 Definitions of Love, according to Urban Dictionary," Thought Catalog, April 4, 2016, https://thoughtcatalog.com/marisa donnelly/2016/04/36-definitions-of-love-according-to-urban-dictionary/.
2. John Naisbitt and Patricia Aburdene, *Megatrends 2000: Ten New Directions for the 1990's* (New York: Morrow, 1990), 16.
3. Yang Claire Yang et al., "Social Relationships and Physiological Determinants of Longevity across the Human Life Span," *Proceedings of the National Academy of Sciences* 113, no. 3 (2016): 201511085, https://www.pnas.org/content/pnas/113/3/578.full.pdf?-b028-4462-9bf9-ba6=.
4. Krystine I. Batcho, "What Will Your Children Remember about You?," *Psychology Today*, June 18, 2015, https://www.psychologytoday.com/us/blog/longing-nostalgia/201506/what-will-your-children-remember-about-you-0.
5. William Harms, "AAAS 2014: Loneliness Is a Major Health Risk for Older Adults," UChicago News, February 16, 2014, https://news.uchicago.edu/story/aaas-2014-loneliness-major-health-risk-older-adults.

Chapter 2: What Is Relational Intelligence?

1. Pamela N. Danziger, "3 Things Retailers Need to Learn from Apple about the Experience Economy," *Forbes*, December 13, 2017, https://www.forbes.com/sites/pamdanziger/2017/12/13/three-things-retailers-need-to-learn-from-apple-about-the-experience-economy/#595680fd1307.
2. Giada Pezzini, "The Apple Store's Secret of Success (and What Retailers Can Learn from It)," *LS Retail Blog*, January 27, 2016, https://www.lsretail.com/blog/ apple-stores-secret-success-retailers-can-learn.
3. Hannah Fry, "'Adulting' Is Hard. UC Berkeley Has a Class for That," *Los Angeles Times*, December 10, 2019, https://www.latimes.com/california/story/2019-12-10/adulting-is-hard-uc-berkeley-has-a-class-for-that.
4. *Merriam-Webster*, s.v. "intelligence," last updated December 5, 2020, https://www.merriam-webster.com/dictionary/intelligence. Emphasis added.

Chapter 3: The First Element of Relational Intelligence: Secure Attachment

1. Sue Johnson with Kenneth Sanderfer, *Created for Connection: The "Hold Me Tight" Guide for Christian Couples* (New York: Little, Brown and Company, 2016), 25.
2. Robert Karen, *Becoming Attached: First Relationships and How They Shape Our Capacity to Love* (New York: Oxford University Press, 1998).
3. Joanne Kuller, "The Power of Touch and Hugs for Babies," Nurse.com https://resources.nurse.com/the-power-of-touch-and-hugs-for-babies and

https://www.ncbi.nlm.nih.gov/pmc/articles/PMC2844909/.

Randomized, controlled studies have documented greater weight gain in preterm newborns receiving moderate pressure massage therapy (see Field, Hernandez-Reif & Freedman, 2004; Vickers, Ohlsson, Lacy & Horsley, 2004 for reviews). These include our studies on preterm newborns who received 5–10 days of massage therapy and showed a 21–48% greater increase in weight gain and hospital stays of 3–6 days less than control infants (Diego, Field & Hernandez-Reif, 2005; Dieter, Field, Hernandez-Reif, Emory & Redzepi, 2003; Field, Schanberg, Scafidi, Bauer & Vega-lahr, 1986; Scafidi, Field, Schanberg, Bauer & Vega-Lahr, 1990; Wheeden, Scafidi, Field, Ironson & Valdeon, 1993) . . . These weight-gain findings have been replicated by at least 4 independent groups (Cifra & Sancho, 2004; De-Roiste & Bushnell, 1996; Goldstein-Ferber, Kuint, Weller, Feldman, Dollberg, Arbel & Kohelet, 2002; Mathai, Fernandez, Modkar & Kanbur, 2001).

4. James A. Coan and David A. Sbarra, "Social Baseline Theory: The Social Regulation of Risk and Effort," *Current Opinion in Psychology* 1 (2015): 87–91, https://doi.org/10.1016/j.copsyc.2014.12.021.

5. Jean-Philippe Gouin et al., "The Influence of Anger Expression on Wound Healing," *Brain, Behavior, and Immunity* 22, no. 5 (2008): 699–708, https://doi.org/10.1016/j.bbi.2007.10.013.

Chapter 4: The Second Element of Relational Intelligence: Fearless Exploration

1. Winston S. Churchill, *The Story of the Malakand Field Force* (London: Longman, 1898), 107.

2. Kenneth Ginsburg, quoted in Lisa Pevtzow, "Kids Given Free Range to Explore Their World," *Chicago Tribune*, January 16, 2013, https://www.chicagotribune.com/news/ct-xpm-2013-01-16-ct-x-0116-free-range-kids-20130116-story.html.

3. Tom Junod, "Can You Say . . . Hero?," *Esquire*, April 6, 2017, https://www.esquire.com/entertainment/tv/a27134/can-you-say-hero-esq1198/.

4. Pevtzow, "Kids Given Free Range to Explore Their World."

Chapter 5: The Third Element of Relational Intelligence: Unwavering Resilience

1. Abby Ellin, "Special Report: Why Developing Resilience May Be the Most Important Thing You Can Do for Your Well-Being Right Now," *Everyday Health*, April 6, 2020, https://www.everydayhealth.com/wellness/state-of-resilience/.

2. Dean M. Becker, quoted by Diane Coutu in "How Resilience Works," *Harvard Business Review*, May 2002, https://hbr.org/2002/05/how-resilience-works.

3. S. M. Southwick and D. S. Charney, "Ready for Anything," *Scientific American Mind* 24, no. 3 (2013): 32, https://doi.org.dts.idm.oclc.org/10.1038/scientificamericanmind0713-32.

4. Ellin, "Special Report."

5. Lenore Skenazy, "School Cancels Beach Trip for Fear of Sunshine," Free-Range Kids, June 24, 2016, https://www.freerangekids.com/school-cancels-beach-trip-for-fear-of-sunshine/.

6. Jenni Fink, "Teacher Claims She Was Fired for Violating 'No Zero' Policy by Not Giving Credit to Students Who Didn't Turn In Project," *Newsweek*,

September 25, 2018, https://www.newsweek.com/teacher-claims-she-was-fired-violating-no-zero-policy-not-giving-students-who-1137573.

7. "Time for Parents to Power Down: Why Coddling Children Can Harm Them," *The Chronicle of Higher Education*. University of Warwick. January 27, 2019, https://www.chronicle.com/paid-article/time-for-parents-to-power-down/212.

Chapter 6: The Fourth Element of Relational Intelligence: Wise Decision-Making

1. Ray Corrado and Jeffrey Mathesius, "Developmental Psycho- Neurological Research Trends and Their Importance for Reassessing Key Decision-Making Assumptions for Children, Adolescents, and Young Adults in Juvenile/Youth and Adult Criminal Justice Systems," *Bergen Journal of Criminal Law and Criminal Justice* 2, no. 2 (2014): 141–63, https://doi.org/10.15845/bjclcj.v2i2.707.

2. Robert S. Boyd, "Teenagers Can't Think Straight, Scientists Say," *Orlando Sentinel*, December 21, 2006, https://www.orlandosentinel.com/news/os-xpm-2006-12-21-teenbrains21-story.html.

3. Laurence Steinberg, "A Social Neuroscience Perspective on Adolescent Risk-Taking," *Developmental Review* 28, no. 1 (2008): 78–106, https://doi.org/10.1016/j.dr.2007.08.002.

4. Torkel Klingberg, *The Overflowing Brain: Information Overload and the Limits of Working Memory* (Oxford: Oxford University Press, 2009).

5. Richard L. Byyny, "Information and Cognitive Overload: How Much Is Too Much?," *Pharos Alpha Omega Alpha Honor Med Soc* 79, no. 4 (2016): 2–7.

6. Moshe Bar, "Think Less, Think Better," *New York Times*, June 17, 2016, https://www.nytimes.com/2016/06/19/opinion/sunday/think-less-think-better.html.

Chapter 7: The Fifth Element of Relational Intelligence: Future-Focused Service

1. Kira Newman, "The Surprisingly Boring Truth about Millennials and Narcissism," Greater Good Science Center, January 17, 2018, https://greatergood.berkeley.edu/article/item/the_surprisingly_boring_truth_about_millennials_and_narcissism.

2. Neil Howe and William Strauss, *Millennials Rising: The Next Great Generation* (New York: Vintage Books, 2000).

3. Peter Koczanski and Harvey S. Rosen, "Are Millennials Really Particularly Selfish? Preliminary Evidence from a Cross-Sectional Sample in the Philanthropy Panel Study," *American Behavioral Scientist* 63, no. 14 (2019): 1965–82, https://doi.org/10.1177/0002764219850871.

4. Nancy J. Hanson-Rasmussen and Kristy J. Lauver, "Environmental Responsibility: Millennial Values and Cultural Dimensions," *Journal of Global Responsibility* 9, no. 1 (2018): 6–20, https://doi.org/10.1108/JGR-06-2017-0039.

5. Martin Luther King Jr., "The Drum Major Instinct," sermon delivered at Ebenezer Baptist Church, Atlanta, February 4, 1968, https://kinginstitute.stanford.edu/king-papers/documents drum-major-instinct-sermon-delivered-ebenezer-baptist-church.

6. Martta Kelly, "The Trick to Getting Your Kids to Help around the House," Live Science, April 30, 2014, https://www.livescience.com/45240-getting-kids-help-cleaning.html.

Chapter 9: Three Currents That Can Stop You from Becoming Relationally Intelligent

1. Deborah E. Gorton, *Embracing Uncomfortable: Facing Our Fears While Pursuing Our Purpose* (Chicago: Northfield Publishing, 2020), 107.

Chapter 10: Three Gifts to Succeed in Modeling and Coaching Relational Intelligence

1. Santiago Ramon y Cajal, *Cajal's Degeneration and Regeneration of the Nervous System,* (London: Oxford University Press, 1928).
2. Moheb Costandi, *Neuroplasticity* (Cambridge, MA: MIT Press, 2016), 95.
3. Philippe Douyon, *Neuroplasticity: Your Brain's Superpower: Change Your Brain and Change Your Life* (Salt Lake City: Izzard Ink, 2019), 16, 26.
4. Costandi, *Neuroplasticity*, 95.

YOUR CHILD IS SMART, BUT DOES HE OR SHE *BELIEVE* IT?

HOW TO RAISE A GODLY MAN,
NOT A FULL-GROWN BOY.

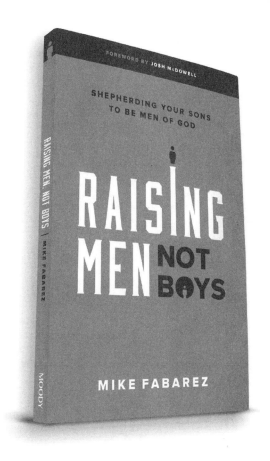

Raising Men, Not Boys is about navigating the times and raising a generation of men on godly principles—sons who are ready, able, and motivated to represent God during their days of sojourn on this earth. Parents will be equipped to set the spiritual trajectory of sons so that they launch into godly manhood, rather than flounder in prolonged immaturity.

978-0-8024-1657-5 | also available as an eBook